Mr. G. HEYWOOD HILL.   SNAPE PRIORY,   SAXMUNDHAM.   SUFFOLK
SNAPE 233
28 Dec.68

Many thanks for card.   The   s that
my desk - failing any   deep
in drift so that   :h
day you sugge   nch
(both of you).   ave
been 1st Sunda   hat -
or any followin   give a
day's notice if   Lucy and
all children did   ill yesterday so
our Christmas wa   it late but now we are
in the thick of it.   Hoping to see you
and all stigamata (I shall leave that extra
A - it somehow helps).

     Happy New Year & love from the Prior,
Prioress and all the nuns   Heywood

to learn that H.J.
was mad about the
name SAXMUNDHAM.
     Anne and I are off
to-morrow to stay with
Mairi Bury at Mount Stewart.
Betty Batten will be there
also, I believe, Derek Hill
and Robin McD. - so what
with petrol bombs as well -
it will be a real hinder
         If we survive
                London
                        Heywood

A SPY IN THE
BOOKSHOP

*Letters between Heywood Hill
and John Saumarez Smith 1966–74*

A SPY IN THE BOOKSHOP

Letters between Heywood Hill
and John Saumarez Smith 1966–74

EDITED BY JOHN SAUMAREZ SMITH

FRANCES LINCOLN

A SPY IN THE BOOKSHOP

Frances Lincoln Limited
4 Torriano Mews
Torriano Avenue
London NW5 2RZ
www.franceslincoln.com

First Frances Lincoln edition: 2006

ISBN 10: 0 7112 2698 9
ISBN 13: 978 0 7112 2698 2

Printed in England

2 4 6 8 9 7 5 3 1

CONTENTS

INTRODUCTION

I first heard of Heywood Hill's bookshop in July 1963 at a family wedding when Heywood Jr, the bookseller's nephew, married my first cousin, Jenny Lipscomb. Later that year, after four terms as an undergraduate, I visited the shop in early December and offered my extra pair of hands as a Christmas slave. During the gap between Winchester and Cambridge, I had spent three months working at Heffers, the University's main bookshop, and in a callow way I thought I could be useful in another bookshop. Handasyde Buchanan, Heywood's partner and contemporary, put me right very quickly, particularly when I mentioned my connection with the Hill family. I was sent packing.

In early 1965 I started looking for a permanent job and was interviewed by two distinguished publishers, Mervyn Horder of Duckworth, and Victor Gollancz. Sir Victor thought that, because he had known and admired my maternal grandfather, I could be trained as his protégé, but I turned down his invitation during a memorable lunch at the Savoy Grill. My uncle John Raven, then the Senior Tutor of King's College, Cambridge, had told me that Heywood Hill was looking for a young apprentice, ready to learn the trade, and had given me Mr Buchanan's full name and address. I was summoned to meet him and he took me round to 39 Charles Street where his friend Michael Stanley had a top-floor flat. I was given a well-prepared grilling. He followed this by taking up a reference with the University Appointments Board. The next time he saw me, he said that he now knew everything about me ("like a butterfly on a board") and he offered me the job, starting in September.

In the previous year Heywood had made plans to sell the business. He had heard that Henry Vyner, wealthy and well connected, had bought the major share of Marlborough Rare Books in Bond Street and would be happy to combine the two bookshops. This was duly achieved, but the Buchanans, who had not been consulted, made no secret of their displeasure. Heywood was to work full-time until the end of August 1965. Thereafter he would appear two days a week and devote himself to buying and selling prints. During the summer of 1965, the shop had gone through a considerable refurbishment. Heywood's desk by the window disappeared, new folio shelves were installed and a handsome plan-chest was made for the Print Room downstairs. Handy's desk remained in the same central position next to the fireplace, but it acquired a second telephone to sit alongside the old Bakelite model which survived until the 1990s. The shop was completely re-wired and repainted.

When I first arrived, I was given a neat desk opposite the (then) front door. Handy introduced me to Liz Forbes at the back of the shop, to Diana Dykes, the shop's secretary who also looked after the children's books, and to Mr Stafford, the full-time packer. Mollie Buchanan did not appear until Wednesday. She was no longer working, as she had done as the book-keeper five days a week, but spent two days writing shop bills at home and a day and a half sitting opposite Liz at the desk at the back.

Heywood had first opened his own bookshop at 17 Curzon Street in 1936 after serving a seven-year apprenticeship with Charles Sawyer in Grafton Street. Lady Anne Gathorne-Hardy worked as his first assistant and they married two years later. When Heywood was called up in late 1942, Nancy Mitford had been employed by him for about seven months. This period was vividly described in *A Bookseller's War*, the letters exchanged between Heywood and

Anne from December 1942 until Anne stopped working in the following April. By then, Mollie Friese-Green was doing the accounts; Nancy and she combined to run the business until 1945. The move from 17 to 10 Curzon Street happened in 1943. There was no major change in the staff after Liz was recruited in 1946.

Handasyde ("Handy") Buchanan worked for Michael Williams' bookshop at 3 Curzon Street between 1930 and 1940, when the premises received a direct hit from a bomb. He was in Press Censorship for most of the war and was invited to join Heywood's shop in 1945. He and Mollie married in 1949, much to the surprise of Heywood and Anne, and Handy was given 20 per cent of the shop's equity in 1960.

Heywood, Handy and Liz each had their own customers – very broadly: highbrow, middlebrow and lowbrow. I was now expected to inherit and cherish Heywood's customers. There was a strong competitive feeling between the different camps. Handy made no secret of his loathing of the works of Henry James nor of his acute state of boredom induced by subjects like music, Victoriana or children's books. In the London trade he was the acknowledged expert on flower and bird books, with a particular line in Thornton's *Temple of Flora*. He had been involved in writing bibliographies, *Fine Bird Books* (1953) and *Great Flower Books* (1956), and had helped to create two or three splendid collections. His regular customers read military history, biographies and memoirs, books on cricket and railways, anything to do with Sherlock Holmes, and novels by his contemporaries and friends, Graham Greene, Evelyn Waugh and, of course, Nancy Mitford. He never knew that Waugh had once written to Nancy that he (Handy) had "the concealed malice of the underdog".

Liz read three or four novels or thrillers a week. She ordered most of the shop's fiction and was supplied with steady streams of proof copies by publishers. Several of her customers read as much, and as quickly, as she did, and depended entirely on her judgement. If she was away from the shop, her customers simply waited to buy their books until she returned. It was several years after her departure from the shop before I read favourite authors of hers such as Dick Francis or Ian Fleming. She had great enthusiasm, but it tended to be reserved for her friends.

Most customers had accounts. When they bought their books, Handy would scribble titles and prices on scruffy pieces of paper and these would be transcribed into the Day Book. From there Mollie would transfer the totals to her four shop ledgers, divided A–D, E–K, L–Q and R–Z. Every regular customer had a page of their own, with their name and address at the top. They were the shop's establishment, below which there was a wide range of occasional customers known as Sundries. A Sundry could be promoted to a page account, a promotion decided on Mollie's whim. Hand-written bills went out every three months with the book-keeper working gradually through the alphabet. Customers who had not received bills for some weeks would sometimes ask when they might expect to pay and would be reassured that Mollie was just approaching the letter S, for instance, and that a bill would be sent in the next few days.

If the process appears to have involved a great deal of writing, it did provide several checks for accuracy. In writing these titles and prices, we impressed their details on our memories. Without a trained memory life would have been intolerable: even after forty years I remember a large proportion of the books published during this particular period, as well as the full addresses of most of the regular customers. No one compiled a card index of these details until after Handy had retired.

Liz looked after the Order Book for new books. In it she wrote customers' names, the books they wanted and the date the order was recorded at the publisher. The book was handed on to the secretary in the middle of every morning for the orders to be rung through to publishers' trade counters: John Murray in Clerkenwell, William Collins in Glasgow, Heinemann in Smart's Mews or the dreaded Book Centre in Southport. Only during Liz's holidays did anyone else handle her Order Book. During the rest of the year she fielded a steady stream of confusing names and figures: no wonder she could be short-tempered.

If customers wanted second-hand books, their orders went into the Clique book. Heywood looked after this for many years, and I took it on. *The Clique* was a weekly magazine which circulated in the second-hand book trade: it contained no editorial matter, only booksellers' advertisements, sometimes arranged in alphabetical order. Once our advertisement was printed, we were sent quotations by provincial dealers ("We can quote – Buchan: John Macnab. Nelson, 1941. Red cloth, pocket edition. 7/6") to which we responded with a postcard ("Please send – John Macnab. 7/6"). Because we were decisive and paid our bills on the nail, we were popular with both regular and occasional suppliers and, in tracing anything out of print, had a high success rate.

Soon after my first arrival, I was introduced to Henry Vyner, the new owner. He was probably about ten years older than I was, and appeared easy-going. Handy expected him to ask me searching questions. This prompted Henry, who had been at Eton and Cambridge himself, to wonder why, after an expensive education, I wanted to work in a shop. I told him that I'd always liked bookshops, that I'd had a spell working in Heffers and that Heywood Hill seemed special. "Good," he said, "I just wanted you to know that I have never done a day's turn and I never intend to do one. If you were running the shop at some future time, I would be a sleeping partner." This did not bode well, any more than his incredibly limp handshake.

Existing facts about the bookshop percolated through to me only by inference. No one explained the state of warfare between the Hills and the Buchanans, later referred to as The Shop Row. When he sold the business, Heywood seemed unaware that Handy would be paid 20 per cent of the proceeds. Over many years, both Handy and Mollie had felt critical of his business acumen, and had bullied him with persistent small-mindedness. Heywood realized that the bookshop would collapse without both of them and, as his sixtieth birthday approached, felt that he had had enough. He would live in Suffolk, surrounded by his family, and hope to stay in touch with the bookish friends he had made in the shop. Handy was to be given a new, generous contract of employment and Mollie would work part-time. For the Buchanans, this sale was treachery of the blackest degree. They would have liked to choose an owner for themselves; instead, they would be spending the final years of their working lives under someone unsympathetic. Liz Forbes sided with the Buchanans.

In 1966 Henry Vyner, a gambler on a frightening scale, was forced to sell his vast Studley Royal estate in Yorkshire. He had used it as security for a dubious business deal and the estate had to go, including Fountains Abbey and forty tenant farms. Those who came to the auction were instructed that they could not be given credit, they must settle in cash, speed was of the essence. This had repercussions in Curzon Street. If Henry could lose so much, what might he stake, perhaps on the turn of a card, next time? Might we find one day that we belonged to someone from the Clermont Club in Berkeley

Square? The Buchanans needed to contact their solicitor to make sure that this could never happen.

Handy regarded himself as a complete professional, in contrast to Heywood, the charming, but bumbling, amateur. He had been educated at Rugby and University College, Oxford. After he graduated, he had spent eighteen months in the City before joining Michael Williams, where "from the word go I could read a balance sheet". Just after the 1929 crash, bookselling was hard: few customers, doubtful profits and a very small salary. Nevertheless he persevered and, at a time when antiquarian books on birds and flowers were on the market but undervalued, he made himself into an expert. He examined and collated the fine folios at auction and, as soon as he found collectors needing advice, he began to buy on their behalf or, if the price was right, for his own stock. He combined scholarship, which was then unfindable in printed form, with a hard-headed enthusiasm. He felt that it was important to specialize and that books with plates by Ehret, Redouté and Gould would always be valued and collected.

A creature of habit, he liked opening the shop at 8.30 a.m. but kept the door closed while he went round the tables and saw what had been sold on the previous day. He swore by a regime of an apple for breakfast, presumably with something more substantial to sustain him until his departure to the pub at 11.30. He liked walking round Shepherd Market. He would don his hat, coat and scarf in mid-morning and mid-afternoon to take the air and, possibly, clear his mind. The half-hour after his lunch, which was largely liquid, was the worst possible time for colleagues or customers to ask him any questions. He suffered from natural dyspepsia but told anyone who enquired about his health that he was a martyr to diverticulitis.

He liked to think of himself as a ladies' man. His wife

Mollie was constantly warning him against looking untidy or unkempt. His hair was cut or brushed at least once a week at Trumper's next door. His dark suits ("you must always dress at least as well as your customers") had to be made for him because he had a slightly humped back. He wore an Old Rugbeian tie every working day, once admitting that he kept thirty-five identical ties in differing conditions which he used in rotation. A quack had told him that he should wear two pairs of hand-knitted woollen socks to ensure that his feet would never sweat. Short-sighted at an early age, he needed thick-lensed spectacles and, on account of his socialist principles, chose National Health frames. I was rash enough on one occasion to suggest that his optician might improve on these frames and was firmly told that his spectacles were an important element of his image and would under no circumstances be changed.

Handy and Mollie play the leading parts in the letters that follow. They cared passionately about the success of the bookshop and had devoted a great part of their lives to its continuation. In fact, it was central to their marriage and their social life. Mollie's character may be thought to have emerged from the blacker areas of my imagination. Once Heywood had retired and Handy was running the shop, she had more chance to exert her malignant jealousy. She was a tall, handsome woman who dressed very well. She had stagnant eyes which reflected no light and a voice that was clipped and calculating. But the customers never saw her in action. She would wait until the shop was empty before she released her poison and, if the front door should re-open, her teeth would clamp shut. I was assured that she had friends and that she could be charming company. For the staff at Heywood Hill, she was an unholy terror.

The reader might ask why I stayed the course. While editing this correspondence, I have sometimes wondered myself. There were other jobs to be had in bookselling and publishing. On the other hand, I had originally been chosen as the person to succeed Handy when he retired. The bookshop had an extraordinary reputation and a cross-section of loyal and interesting customers. When I started writing to Heywood, I'd already had a year of observing his influence over his friends, and had seen him as a kindred spirit. When reporting anecdotes and conversations to him, they were fresh in my mind and, by sharing them, I was getting them off my own chest. Once described, they no longer preyed on my impressionable mind. If they amused Heywood and Anne, so much the better. If friends of the Buchanans are surprised, I admit that Heywood and I probably encouraged each other to dwell on their shortcomings.

The letters cover a period of eight years. They may give the impression that working at Heywood Hill was constantly stressful. This would be misleading because my exchange with Heywood represents a single facet of a diverse, and often diverting, life. It may not have been typical of the period of the late sixties, but it had considerable rewards, literary and social. Through the shop I had a huge acquaintance and customers often became friends. I had never lived in London before 1965 and could explore new areas, new museums, new bookshops at will. If I had an early proof copy of a novel or biography, I read it with shop customers in mind. They liked to have books recommended to them and were grateful if they enjoyed what the shop sold them. This particularly applied to presents. "Have you read this?" the customer would ask. "Would it suit my mother/nephew/god-daughter?" We were matching books with people and making instant judgements on character and personality; we must have made occasional mistakes. But we were constantly on the look-out for good books. The publishers, most of whom we knew, were obviously pleased when we gave a generous order, based on our having read a proof in advance. I recently came across a letter from Richard Ollard, then at William Collins, thanking Handy for ordering so many copies of Sybille Bedford's *Aldous Huxley*. In fact, Handy couldn't have been less interested and he passed the letter on to me. Once the book was published, with strict rules that it should not be displayed until the day of publication, we closely followed the reactions of the leading reviewers. *Aldous Huxley* was given rough treatment in the *TLS* on the grounds that the biographer was not academically objective and showed too clearly her friendship with Maria Huxley. When one of "our" books won a literary prize, we felt as if we'd backed a winner in the Grand National.

In some respects the attitude to good new books has not changed. In other ways, in the relationship between publisher and bookseller, in the role of the reps and in the existence of wholesalers and chain bookshops, not to speak of the internet, the picture is unrecognisable. But this is not the right context in which to praise times past. Some of our accepted customs would now seem extraordinary, such as our regular disposal of unwanted books. This will always be a problem for a new bookshop, however efficient its system or management. In the sixties we were telephoned every four months or so by a Mr Rosen who had a stall in a north London street market. Had we got enough for him to take away at a shilling a book? Yes, the piles on the floor were looking rather higher than usual, we could do some culling, and we'd look forward to seeing him on Saturday. So Mr R., a burly redhead in an alpaca jacket, would appear, carry seventy or eighty books out to a taxi, regularly complain that he couldn't sell hardback novels, and pay us what he owed. We needed the space, he wanted cheap books, everyone was happy.

It was when I was first reading Heywood's letters to Nancy Mitford in the Chatsworth archive that I was reminded of my early correspondence with him. Heywood had sworn Nancy to secrecy, and had never told me himself that he was quoting to her large chunks of my letters over a period of five or six years. Once the editing had been completed and *The Bookshop at 10 Curzon Street* published, I thought I should contact Anne Hill and ask whether my original letters had survived or if they had been part of a large archival confection sold to the Lilly Library in Bloomington, Indiana. Back came a reply that they had not been included. Knowing that I'd kept Heywood's letters, Anne encouraged me to put the two together as a sequel. The result is necessarily more subjective than the first book, and may be over-revealing. It might be subtitled "The Education of a Bookseller".

John Saumarez Smith
June 2006

NOTE TO THE READER

Handasyde Buchanan was universally called Handy, but Heywood sometimes referred to him as the Pope or Crafty. In his more headmasterly role he was EHB.

Mollie signed herself CMB, but in the letters she became the Red Queen, the Countess, the Witch and the Head Matron.

Together, they were the Bs or the Bucks.

See also Biographical Index, page 171.

As in *The Bookshop at 10 Curzon Street,* I have omitted the tops and tails of letters and mentioned an address only when it is not our respective home. Heywood was writing from Snape Priory, Saxmundham, Suffolk; I from 102 Wendover Court, Chiltern Street, London W1 until October 1970 when we moved to 28 Canonbury Place, London N1.

1966

H.H. left the shop at the beginning of September. By the
16th, after a week's holiday, I was writing a postcard to him
apologizing for not sending him a letter full of news, but
"rather selfishly preferred to keep the bitterness out of my
mind". He must have replied because, three days later, I was
thanking him for his letter, which gave me heart enough ...

J.S.S. 19/9/66

... to cope with rebuffs which never materialized ... I can
only see storm clouds looming over Wednesday when the two
women [Mollie Buchanan and Liz Forbes] will be facing each
other. I suppose I've been through it all before, but there is so
little need for it that one always hopes it may be better this
once – particularly when I've had a week in common-or-
garden human society outside the shop.

I'm afraid I'm not going to expand on the Bitterness – it
somehow seems degrading to deal in the same currency as the
Buchanans ... There was the most appalling fuss over your
party[1] for a day or two, but the Bs preferred to keep the affair
to themselves, and Liz and I were less-than-amused onlook-
ers. I had to come clean very soon because Mollie had leapt to
the conclusion that [the party] was happening on your initia-
tive, and I couldn't bear to hear this bruited around. It was
boring that the newspapers caught onto it, because some of
their readers reckoned the shop was closing. There was some
predictable gibbering about these rumours ... but I'm very
glad the party went well – I wish I could have been there.

---

1. One of Heywood's oldest friends, Robin McDouall (1908–85), arranged a
party in Heywood's honour at the Travellers' Club, Pall Mall.

Rather spurred by the arrival of my youngest brother's school magazine,[2] I've been thinking about St Heywoods (better than Heywood Hall/House, tho' these sound very plausible) and its mag. for '65–'66. "Boys and girls will be welcome," it could start, "on all weekdays and on Saturday morning. They will be greeted by the headmaster, the matron or the junior master. The headmaster's wife will receive visitors on Wednesdays and on Friday afternoon, but visitors should be wary of their manners and should respect her status with care. Prefects and their immediate friends are excused from this convention."[3]

I don't quite see how to continue. We could produce a pretty fair collection of literary efforts by the school during the year, not forgetting a composition or two from E[lizabeth] F[orbes]. . . . Not too easy to see the school having much of an athletic record, which is essential to the best prep schools, tho' I fancy Lord Hardwicke[4] probably plays a powerful game of polo and Mrs Montefiore[5] might have a dazzling past on the lacrosse field. And if I'd been careful enough to note down some of the year's funnies, we could include a column of Heywoodiana . . .

Very best wishes for your holiday and I'll look forward to putting on my disguise in November.

---

2. My brother Charles (b. 1954), now Director of the National Gallery, was at St Ronan's prep school in Hawkhurst, Kent.
3. I suggested twelve of the shop's best customers as school prefects, including Paul Mellon, the Duke of Devonshire, George Cukor (the Hollywood film director) and Noël Coward.
4. Lord Hardwicke (1906–74) was a dashing figure in West End society, handsomely suited with a fresh carnation in his buttonhole.
5. Mrs Ruth Sebag-Montefiore (b. 1916), sister of Sir Philip Magnus, biographer. She had worked in publishing in her youth.

H.H.   26/9/66   Knockhill House, by Newport, Fife

I was VERY pleased and amused by your letter. Brilliant
about St Heywood's. There is only one thing which I think
you missed in the mag. It is believed that, on Founder's Day,
the Saint himself will float through the school on a cloud.
That will bring immense pleasure to the pupils as it is known
that the headmaster's wife will be bringing her bow and her
vast supply of arrows.

It is a strange anomaly that a co-ed – and therefore, I
suppose, a prog. School – should be such a Dotheboys Hall.
Do be careful not to catch the team spirit. I don't believe you
will but it is very infectious.

I have been going through the Lambes' books,[6] some of
which she wants to sell. I had thought of writing to Handy
about the best of them but there has lately been some mysterious disorder by which a great many of them have become
damaged by damp. There is a Pine's Horace in contemp.
Morocco, an 1802 col. plate book on Africa, first editions of
Brontë, Disraeli and Yeats, and a great many Private Press
books. As, when I do write to him about books, it will be
something in the nature of a test case, I think that I shall wait
till I can report ones which he might be keen about . . .

If Mollie has not yet had her holiday, I'd be grateful for a
postcard to say when it is. I might then venture to have my
hair cut in Curzon St.

J.S.S.   28/9/66

The headmaster's wife will be away from tomorrow (Sept
29th) to October 3rd, and October 5th to 10th. The school
would welcome a visit from the Saint himself, tho' pupils

---

6. Lady (Peta) Lambe, a longstanding friend of Heywood and widow of
Admiral Sir Charles Lambe.

must forego the pleasure [for the time being] of seeing him
branded, barbed or toasted.

J.S.S.   28/10/66

Can you possibly help to tie up a loose thread? You gave a
book to Wessely [bookbinder] in June to be bound for a
friend of mine called Howarth.[7] He did the binding according
to his records at the very beginning of July; he probably
returned the book in mid-July. There is no trace of the binding
operation in any of our books – and, of course no sign of the
book (Aigon: *Les Années des Aventures de Louis Philippe*).
Do you remember at all? I feel stricken with guilt as it was
being bound for the Howarth father who was my house-
master at school, and I don't want the shop to appear as a
model of incompetence. How can it have slipped through all
the nets without record?

H.H.   29/10/66

Most sorry to say that I cannot help over that book. I have
no recollection of it whatever. If I was guilty, the only possible
sin which I can think I might have committed is to have sent
the book to my cousin Johnstone (Miss E.) in Cornwall.
Nearly all the books which I had done by Wessely were hers.
She has a huge library and I was slowly repairing it. I think it
unlikely, however, as she is one of those methodists who keeps
a list of all the titles she sends . . .

I have been meaning to write to you to suggest a date for
your visit. Since Anne and I got back [from holiday], grandchildren have been showered on us. My m. in law's cook has
declared that she will be away next weekend, so Anne will
have to take her place. On 7th we are going away for a week.

---

7. Alan Howarth (b. 1944), now Lord Howarth of Newport.

So all that, I fear, means no chance until 18th Nov onwards . . ., but I suddenly remember with horror that that begins to be the period when the headmaster vetoes all exeats. There is a 6.30 train which you could catch on Friday evening. If that is not permitted, there is a 1.30 on Saturday. I might be able to meet you at Ipswich which saves a bit of fare (there is nobody here to tip). You can spend as long as you like in bed of a morning which I mention in case you find it essential after school hysterics . . . Don't be daunted by the hurdles.

My next letter (6 November) includes a long pastiche of a fairy story in the style of a collection of Greek legends made by R. M. Dawkins. It dealt with a king who needed an heir and a boy, Yanni, who set out on a long and painful journey to a hill where he would find the Lamp of Life. Buchanan-like monsters also figured.

    On the subject of a weekend in Suffolk, it seemed more sensible to wait until after Christmas.

H.H.   19/11/66

I was rather appalled to get a letter from my cousin to say that she had been into the shop and announced she had not got Louis Philippe. She is such a tactless woman that she probably did it in the crudest way which I do hope did not reverberate on to you. The period of blood sweat and tears must be beginning to stream and you won't want to have any extra horror thrown in. I really don't think that I can have done anything improper with that book . . . there's no chance, I suppose, that it could be done up in the packing room?

I don't expect that I will be able to bring myself to look in again at the old school before Christmas. It does require quite a lot of bringing, I find, and the Head is always so obviously pre-occupied and it would only add to that stream.

H.H   2/12/66

I had already written you a letter about Osbert [Sitwell] and Balmoral[8] to the shop when yours arrived this morning [this has been lost]. Thought I would send it off all the same. I hoped that by enclosing cash it would save the embarrassment of Day Bookery, though I can see that there's nothing I can do which will stop me being thought treasonable. I did nothing to cause Osbert's defection myself – told no tales out of school – it was the article which did it, helped, I suspect, by tattle of friends.[9]

The latest arrow, aimed last week, was my bill with no discount taken off (Handy had agreed that I should have some. I enclosed a restrained little note when I paid it but am not expecting any result). I've written to Malcolm Bullock's daughter to try to soothe her about not getting an answer about her books. I realize that there's no hope now till after Christmas. She hasn't answered me so I expect she's cross. I shall learn very soon not to sell to or buy from the shop, which is what I suppose is intended. Best really to cut oneself off from the little wounds of petty spite – though I can't help feeling saddened.

Life here is very pleasant – though it makes me feel guilty telling you so. Plenty to do what with trying to prevent too much hard house-keeping falling upon Anne – the cook bolted last week with a negro. The young are often here and the old need just as much looking after . . . Plenty of desk work too

---

8. I had found a nineteenth-century book on Balmoral for Osbert Sitwell to give H.M. The Queen Mother for Christmas.

9. An *Evening Standard* article by Maureen Cleave, Mrs Francis Nichols, several months earlier which had failed to mention Heywood's name in a long interview with Handy. This caused Osbert Sitwell, among other friends of Heywood, to close his shop account.

though too much looking out of the window. I realize that you won't be able to write during this time of agony.

With best survival wishes.

J.S.S.   7/12/66

Another December Wednesday over, thank God! Bad blood's been bubbling all day, and at different times we've each felt like throwing in our hands. I heard a faintly amusing story from Bobbie [Hodgson],[10] who has to put up with as much as any of us, close a friend though he's thought to be. He was round in the Bs' flat discussing details of a buffet supper that he was cooking for Mollie, and was shown the bathroom to admire. M suddenly looked very cross and muttered "O! I haven't changed the loo paper." An incredulous "Oh" from Bobbie as there was some perfectly good paper on the roll. "I always change the paper when I change the towels, and I've forgotten; there are four shades." Not a flicker.

She says she dreams of adding up accounts, and the sums are always right.

She will remember the little fracas last week for some time; if she wasn't bound to, I'd put it straight out of my mind myself. The exchange went like this:

M. That doll's house has always been a menace. Heywood should never have bought it, and anyway should have taken it away from the shop long ago. You do understand? (Pause) How much does it cost?

J. Twelve pounds. I think it's very cheap.

M. (Pause) John, why do you speak so very rudely to me?

J. I'm very sorry. I do get rather rattled by this sort of inquisition.

---

10. Bobbie Hodgson came to the shop one day a week to look after the print business. He took prints to and from our framers, Henry Shemilt in Seymour Place.

M. You're extremely rude, and no one has ever spoken to me in the shop like that before.

J. I'm extremely sorry; I really didn't think I was rude to you. I then go to get my coat as it's my lunch hour. As I return, in order that I should hear:–

M. It's just for that reason that I would like to find someone in the shop in place of you.

J. What did you say?

She repeats.

J. I'm very sorry (in a very small voice, pretty shattered) I had no idea . . . (tail off and exit).

I saw Handy later that afternoon and will be having a long talk this Saturday; I shall pull fewer punches than usual.

I've discovered one point that you will probably find familiar: that the position is in no way improved if you have a comforter at home. Once you start discussing it, petty as it may be, you only increase the worry it causes. My ma was much upset – she knows about the poison and naturally tries to mitigate the lethality – , but I really do better to cope by myself.

I'm having a really good break at Christmas, when I hope to get my nerve back to normal. If only Suffolk wasn't so hugely removed from Oxford where I'll be staying, I'd love to see you and tell all.

H.H.   8/12/66

I got your letter just before starting to London for the day. It was good of you to write during Gethsemane.[11] I was, of course, fascinated. I think it is marvellous how you have endured and do hope that you achieve survival – though often

---

11. For many years the pre-Christmas season at Heywood Hill was known as "Gethsemane".

you must wonder – as I did – if this armour needed against such lunacy isn't too expensive.

I do know what you mean about having someone sympathetic at home. It is easy to become too obsessed by it all but you seem to have a wonderful ability to dismiss it (anyhow, when away from the front), which I don't think I ever managed. In fact, I find that, even back in blighty, I am still bandaging old wounds and puzzling over animal behaviour. How can the Bs have such blind conceit as to build themselves up as pillars of rectitude? Why is M., who is efficient, good-looking and secure, such a tortured woman that she has to leave trails of havoc? How are the Lady Vis[12] so taken in by her? I suppose she has some damned spot which never will out however often she changes the loo paper and cleans the bottoms of carpets . . .

I have specially not been taking my last effects (like unsold doll's houses) away because one of them will, I know, cause major trouble. That is the [round] table by the sacred double desk which Nancy Rodd[13] has given me for a leaving present. I told Handy but it's one of the things he didn't want to hear.[14] . . . I'm writing this in the train which is why it is extra palsied . . .

---

12. Lady Violet Benson (1888–1971) and her husband Guy were particularly cherished friends of the Buchanans.
13. Nancy Mitford (1904–73), who had worked in the shop between 1942 and 1945.
14. See *The Bookshop at 10 Curzon Street*, page 124.

1967

J.S.S.   1/2/67

. . . It looks as if I could catch a train on Friday evening [for a weekend at Snape] – the fortnightly rota hasn't been dished by illness and/or bolshiness as yet . . .

Handy put a superbly characteristic scheme into operation this week and you can imagine the conversations to which it gives rise. On the back half of the round table next to his desk he has his seventeen Favourite Novels of the last 60 years, with a special dispensation for *Diary of a Nobody*. Can you guess them? *Riddle of the Sands, Farewell to Arms* and S. Sassoon's omnibus; *Tono-Bungay* and *Clayhanger; The Wrong Box; Zuleika Dobson, Decline and Fall* and *What's Become of Waring; Forsyte Saga; Anglo-Saxon Attitudes; The Go-Between; Eyeless in Gaza; Loving; The Comedians*; and what can be missing now? The Greatest of All, *Of Human Bondage*. (Pause, while we meditate on the meanings of such a choice.) Of course, to my concealed dismay "the customers are taking it extraordinarily well", and they all turn out to be "very good readers and *very* intelligent". For the first victim or two I feebly muttered that they were perhaps a little gullible, or not outstandingly well-read, but the sad fact emerges that he's made a go of his vanity and he's justified it . . . He had to order the books while Our Lady of the Garden [Elizabeth Forbes] was away last week and he got a red-hot raspberry from her as soon as she returned.

I thought we put on a plausible show of innocence on the evening you called in . . .; as regards keeping our contact dark, we can play the game with confidence and enjoy Life's Little Ironies. The only danger would be from someone like

Rod [Hill][15] in a moment of daftness, or even from Derek [Hill][16] who was in a day or two ago and seemed on the brink of asking some devastating question – I was probably unduly nervous.

H.H. 3/2/67

It is good that there is no impediment to your coming down here on the 24th. No need to bring anything smart as nobody changes for anything. If you'd like a walk, bring shoes that don't matter. As to anonymity, I will give John and Sheila [Hill],[17] if they are here that weekend, a stern lecture . . .

I was of course hugely amused by your description of Handy's Choice. It's *What's Become of Waring*, isn't it, that he makes people read the first page of and then they know at once that they are going to like it. *Anglo-Saxon Attitudes* has always astounded me. It seemed to me a not very good and rather a queer novel which I'd have thought he would think unsuitable. I note that one or two novels, which were declared masterpieces when they appeared, have been dropped.

Perhaps you should each have your booths with your favourite display. How wonderful if they could be sound proof . . . I don't know what M. would have in her booth as I don't think she has any favourites. A little concentration camp maybe . . .

The following Saturday I was submitted to "a most upsetting" interview with Handy. It seemed sensible for me then to appeal to Henry Vyner without Handy knowing.

---

15. Rod was Heywood's nephew, the youngest son of Sheila and John, Heywood's sister and brother-in-law, then living in Aldeburgh.
16. Derek Hill (1918–2000), artist.
17. See note 15.

J.S.S.   9/2/67

Handy probably reckons that he carried off a difficult interview with characteristic triumph – a triumph of will, personality, shrewdness, intelligence, experience . . . He was advising me about my future in the shop – what my contract was going to be, what that meant, and how it affected the firm, the owner and himself. The contract was very much worse that I had been given to expect, a smaller salary than had been promised since the day I arrived, no guarantee that I was to be promoted, and an assurance in so many words that Handy would stay in the shop as long as there was breath in his body. If I'd heard all this from a sympathetic and faintly encouraging viewpoint, I suppose I would have accepted it for what it was, tough but economically necessary (indeed this is just what I had to do on the surface). But Handy is Handy, and he took the chance to tell me exactly how badly I measured up to himself as an ideal, precisely how grateful I should be to him, essentially what a bloody genius he was, and how the shop would collapse without him. I noted down a few scraps of conversation verbatim:–

J. (getting to the end of his tether): If, for the sake of argument, I left the shop here and now, you would surely find it difficult to get somebody to work here instead.

H. Oh no (a beatific smile wreathing his face), surely not. Why?

J. I just think staff pressures are exceedingly tricky and that lots of people would give up straight away.

H. Staff pressures, who do you mean?

J. (No time for pregnant pause) Liz really. Lots of people would find her intolerable.

H. (Pause) No, I don't think you're right about a replacement. Anyone here has got to have something rather extraordinary, but Liz *needn't* be intolerable, I can manage her, so can Mollie. If we had someone absolutely super, Liz would never have a chance. Mollie has always had her completely under her thumb.

J. But that must surely have been the result of very gradual warfare?

H. Not gradual at all: shot her down in flames from the word go.

This represents a comprehensive impasse. Handy's replacement would have to be Handy Mark 2. He suggests that Liz can and should be shot down in flames: who wants to emulate Mollie?

H. If and when you take over, you'll have to deal with people working for you. It won't be easy. Why do you think Mr Stafford[18] stays at his job? It's only because I go down and have a few words with him every day. [Liz] may think it's no good my going round the shop, but that's how the whole place keeps running.

Has Handy any idea what Mr S. thinks of him? He looks back to the days when you were his boss as a golden age. Who wouldn't after a change from benevolent monarchy to constitutional tyranny? . . .

Handy's Favourites will be removed from the table at the end of this week, and will take their place on a newly appointed shelf. It is a measure of his status that no one has really *criticized* his choice, let alone laughed at it. Lord Snow disagrees with *Anglo-Saxon Attitudes* . . . but didn't go further. Most customers were pleased to see such chestnuts in a pile together, and bought them accordingly. Mrs Hardy-Roberts[19] had never seen *Loving* as far as she knew, and was invited to read the first page to see if she liked it (as per *What's*

---

18. Michael Stafford was the shop's packer.
19. Mrs Hardy-Roberts, a regular customer, married to a Brigadier who worked at St James's Palace.

Become of Waring); Richard Smart[20] refused *Tono-Bungay*
for the umpteenth time and the Duke of Kent bought
A Farewell to Arms. . . . Did you notice that not one of the
collection was by a woman? . . .

I'm working on a little bit of nonsense that would start:

Vanity was a very smart engine: his buffers shone, his
boiler glistened and on his top was a little grey smokestack
that he sometimes covered with a brown felt cosy. Even
smarter was his cabin: levers greased, dials transparent,
buttons winking, clock not a minute too fast. "Vanity" was
painted on the side of the engine, but it seemed as if the name
could always be changed: he liked to keep other names ready
for his passengers. Some of them called him "Humility",
others "Stability", yet others "Capability", and there were
even people who had seen "Eccentricity", as bold as brass.
It was a pity that one of his carriages has christened him
"Futility", for that was rather appropriate . . .

I like the idea of Mollie as a tender – a good Latin deriva-
tion – and she'd like carrying all that coal.

H.H.   14/2/67

I have been a few days answering because I was in London
two nights until Sat. and then came back to a tangle of duties
(there are tangles even here, although, except with things like
TAX, the unravelling is usually quite pleasant). I do hope that
your interview with Henry was as satisfactory as could be. I
believe that he is something of a yes-man (although I don't
quite know what that means). I mean that he will agree with
one and then one finds that not a great deal happens . . . I
think Henry is quite shrewd and knows what the Bs are

---

20. Richard Smart, an Australian picture-dealer, particularly well-read in
Henry James.

roughly like – although it takes a long time of daily contact to discover the intricacies of Handy and to see through his bluff-manship and one-upmanships. Hideous words but they suit him. I never told Henry what I really thought because I don't think he wanted to hear. Also I did not want to blight, in Henry's eyes, the genuine quality of Handy's salesmanship and – query – a fundamental kindness in his nature – in spite of the ink Mollie has poured into it. Now I am heading for Cape Horn again so I'd better jib or whatever they do at the Yacht Club. All I'm doing, I realize, is to run through those name-plates on your engine. Still it's quite fun and one can only keep sane by getting some amusement out of it all.

I have had a letter which, if it became known, I think might cause the biggest eruption there has ever been . . . I will tell you when I see you.

Instructions follow about the train he would meet the following week. As a result of his grandchildren staying during the previous few days, "you may find Anne and me a bit battered, and your room may not be so damned spotless as Head matron would desire".

By the time I arrived on 24 February, Heywood and Anne had unearthed a mass of photographs and letters about the shop's history to show me. These led to endless discussions and anecdotes from the past. Most were previously unknown to me: Mollie's background in King's Lynn; her first, failed marriage; her job at a school in Notting Hill patronized by various Hills and Gathorne-Hardys; her marriage to Handy, and the fact that she had been sacked five times by Heywood but had always reappeared the following day as if nothing had changed.

The weekend was memorable for two other reasons. In the middle of Saturday we all went to the Butley Oysterage in Orford for lunch. On the way I asked what I should do if any

*shop customer was also there; it seemed unlikely enough so
far from London, but stranger coincidences have happened.
In fact, an old friend of Handy's, Colonel Ralph Cobbold,[21]
soon sat down at the next door table with his wife and some
friends. Before we left, I approached him and asked him if he
would do me a great favour: when he next came to Heywood
Hill, could he please not mention that he had seen me with
the Hills in Suffolk? If he did, I would get the sack. He
agreed, possibly intrigued by this conspiracy, and never
betrayed me.*

*The second episode happened soon after midnight. I
woke up feeling exceedingly faint. I staggered as far as the
door and fell against the door-jamb, hitting my temple a
fearful crack. Somewhat dazed, I proceeded to the bathroom
where I sat for several minutes. Rather than wake Heywood
and Anne, I then returned to bed where I slept soundly until
morning. By breakfast time I had a considerable egg on the
side of my head, which would need some explaining on
Monday morning.*

*This had never happened to me before and, so far, has
never affected me since.*

J.S.S. to Anne H.   27/2/67

As to the causes of [my fall], I might have caught a germ
which apparently laid Liz low and which wasn't the result of
anything she ate . . . I'd like to think that my parents had been
involved in the Mollificatory witchcraft, as they were also
gossiping about her on Saturday evening. They happened to
meet someone called Mary Goodden who'd worked at Peggy
[Clutten's] school [in Notting Hill] a long time ago: she left
because she couldn't put up with Mollie and she had plenty to

---

21. Colonel Cobbold, then running Justerini and Brooks in St James's Street.

add to the stew-pot. What a shame it is that M. isn't a really old-fashioned witch and we could have her burned; I can somehow see those stagnant eyes of hers surviving the flames till the very last, but the rest would go up a treat – genuine Inflammable Material.

It was a real pleasure to talk and listen about the shop at great length. I do get depressed by Buchanan warfare and there are so few people who know what the warfare means . . . Can I survive? . . . It's worth believing in a Day of Judgement in the strictest O.T. terms . . .

You probably realize how much I enjoyed the weekend. Thank you very very much.

Anne H.   4/3/67

We laughed a lot over [your letter] – but also, John, feel *such* sympathy for you over your predicament in the shop, which we understand so very well. To us, talking to you has been a comfort as well. Heywood, like you, was so many years alone with them in the shop, and when it's 3 to 1, it's so easy to feel (if one is not very conceited) that there must be something wrong with *one* – that one is imagining things or that it is silly to mind so much etc etc . . . I do wish for some turn of the wheel of fate that will make things better for you, and that if you are brave enough to persevere there, you will be rewarded. Write to us if things are intolerable . . .

J.S.S.   15/3/67

I was enormously cheered by Anne's letter: it makes a huge difference to have sympathy from you both . . . After a Wednesday when Mollie was on really wounding form and I happened to be her scapegoat, I couldn't help regretting that you weren't nearer London . . . This morning she referred to my contract as "meaningless, of course, because Handy will retain the right to sack his staff whenever he likes."

Mrs Black[22] took the opportunity to tell Handy this afternoon about the unique qualities of himself and the shop "Thank you very much indeed" purred H. "but when I retire in ten years' time . . ."

H.H.   17/3/67

How vile about last Black Wednesday. Anne and I have long discussions about whether you ought to go on enduring such nastiness and if it wouldn't be better to leave. I now wonder how I can have let it happen to me for 20 years or more. The thing is that it is so despicable that one doesn't want to let oneself be affected by it and on one's stronger days one can sometimes laugh. The cumulative effect, however, is hell. Why not stick for another six months or a year and then, if there's no improvement, tell them some shop truths and leave. If only Henry was less of an enigma and one knew how reliable he would be. . . .

I wrote to Handy about ten days ago saying could I arrange for Green and Abbott[23] to remove my last remains (including the table) and would he have a drink next Tuesday, but no answer. They are of course well-known non-answerers.

I did rather a splendid bit of detective work for Mrs M[ellon].[24] I discovered that the firm whose name she had seen on a ruined sugar cane mill in Antigua with date 1810 is still in existence, and I have written to them and they have

---

22. Mrs Peter Black (1929–2006), a popular and lifelong customer.
23. Green and Abbott, interior decorators in St George Street. For many years it had been run by John Hill, later by his eldest son Nick.
24. Mrs Paul Mellon ("Bunny") had a superb collection of flower books, now at Oak Spring, Upperville, Virginia.

answered saying that they have drawings of some of their early machinery. There hasn't been time to know the result of that yet. Thank goodness it is sugar cane mills and not the temple of flora and all its watery marks. (Not BOOKS is what I mean.)

Will you one day tell me where the Bs are going for their holiday this year? Anne and I have a possibility of ten days in the French Alps at the beginning of July – just their holiday time – and I want to be certain of not going anywhere near or on the same train . . .

PS Eddie was pleased with your Shipwreck letter.[25] I asked him if he was going to order one and he said I don't know yet, my dear. Waiting for Bloomer royalties, I presume.[26] He is yet another well-known non-answerer.

My next letter, written on Easter Monday, was "not an S.O.S., but no one else but you will listen and understand". Henry, Handy and I had met to discuss my salary and contract. Because of previous discussions I had known what each of the others was likely to say, but I'd counted on Henry's support. Instead, he had remained silent and allowed Handy to keep to the meanest possible offer. The result was a compromise. As a concession, I was granted a salary increase from £850 p.a. to £950 p.a. until September when, under a new contract, it would increase to £2,000 p.a. "We had a long and fairly useful talk afterwards about my place in the hierarchy: whether Liz should be allowed to call me an idiot more than 5 times a day, and that sort of thing," but naturally no mention of Mollie.

---

25. I had quoted on a Victorian edition of Falconer's *Shipwreck* to Eddie Gathorne-Hardy.
26. *Adult's Garden of Bloomers*.

*After telling Heywood the Buchanans' dates for their
holiday in Switzerland, I mentioned his letter to Handy about
the table, "which I'd seen among the* relicta *that provoke
customers to ask in two months' time if their letter could
possibly have gone astray. I fear I can do nothing or the Red
Queen will have my head off."*

H.H.   Easter Monday 18/4/67

I am sorry not to have responded sooner to your Easter
Monday letter. We had a delightful time in Cornwall but there
was not a moment of it left over for writing. It seemed to me
that you had "stood up" for yourself most manfully at your
triumvirate . . . without, as you say, telling them where to get
off which would have meant throwing yourself off at the
same time. It's disappointing and baffling about Henry. I had
a drink with him at Brooks's (to tell him of the Mellon letter)
– just before I went away – I think it was the day after the
meeting. He appeared to be thoroughly on your side. The
only criticism he made was that you were "hitting too many
nails on the head". He read Mrs M's letter and seemed unper-
turbed. In fact, he rang me up the next morning and said
would I go and look at a Ms. Flower book at Marlborough[27]
which I might report to her "to give me a start". I went and
looked at it. It was one of those collections on vellum attrib-
uted to nobody and I didn't think that it would be a good
start and told Henry and he gave me one of his hollow laughs.
Bunny (Mrs M.) had rung me up at Sheila [Hill]'s the morning
before from Claridges. I was astounded as had not said where
I was. Also appalled as abhor long telephone talks which is
what she launched on. All about sugar mills in Antigua. She
was properly impressed by my detective work. I asked her if

---

27. Marlborough Rare Books in Bond Street.

she would like me to ring up the firm in Derby. She said YES. I
got on to the manager who said he was just off to London and
would be at the Institute of Public Cleansing all the afternoon. I rang Bunny and told her (she seemed delighted and
shrieked about the Public Cleansing) but after that things
came to an abrupt halt as I discovered . . . that she was going
to have an operation the next day. So I may never know
whether I have revived the sugar cane industry or if I shall get
a reward. She said on the telephone that she would also like
me "to help Jackie Kennedy" (that DID rather impress
Henry). I willingly let myself forget it all in Cornwall, though,
while there, David Batterham[28] wrote to say that his boss had
some interesting early 19th century illustrations for children's
books. That of course would have been JUST the thing
for Bunny and I wrote to David to say so and was deeply
chagrined when he answered that they had been already sold
to LYON.[29] To make matters worse, Booth[30] told Lyon that I
was interested – so, more than likely, that will now all come
booming back. I'm afraid that poor David was dismayed as I
told him he must NOT report things to several people at once.

Henry had the usual old story about the Red Queen – that
she wanted to leave the shop as soon as the new accounts
system began. I told him I had heard that one before. He said
that he thought Handy was liable to become ill at any
moment and would I do some part-time work if he did. I
don't believe in that either (Handy being ill).

I have written this in a rocking train so it is more palsied
than ever . . .

---

28. David Batterham, bookseller, then married to John Hill's daughter Jo.
29. H. D. Lyon (1907–2004), antiquarian bookdealer, unpopular in the
trade.
30. Richard Booth (b. 1938), bookseller, "king" of Hay-on-Wye.

J.S.S.   19/4/67

Delighted to find your letter here when I got back from a wonderful Wednesday . . . I nearly wrote to you again when I had seen Henry for a second time – this time with Handy's official permission . . . but I expected you must be getting bored with the finicky details of my pay and contract.

In general, I'm fairly optimistic about how things are going. It's tempting to sympathise (a little) with Handy about Henry's apathy and cluelessness, and I'm not really confident in Henry's good faith. Partly of course, it's lack of will-power: he will agree with the last person who has spoken to him, and will be equally congenial to all. He knows about finance and antiquarian books and, as far as I can see, he's not prepared to be interested in very much else. It's difficult for him to see the day to day running of the shop because Handy makes him feel very uncomfortable; but sooner or later he'll have to know a bit more than he does or I'll be forced to dictate terms to him in the same way as Handy. This may be what he wants; why after all should a very wealthy man think in terms of six-day weeks? But we *must* cooperate, and I won't stop knocking nails on the head for fear of knocking him . . .

Henry cannot know half the shop troubles if he's suggested that you could step in part-time when Handy's ill. I know he's worried about Handy's illnesses – I can't make out whether diverticulitis is acute constipation or acute gut-rot; Handy only concedes it's acute – , but you would surely never want to come back unless a cataclysm had cleared the air. In the event of the Bs leaving in high dudgeon or otherwise, you would be the only person who could possibly help out. But *not* part time.

The famous new accounts system started on Monday. It was welcomed in the finest style. Liz was very groggy from some sort of tummy upset, Handy and Mollie were having heavy colds (not helped by a weekend with "darling Lettie"[31]), and Mr Stafford left the shop without a word at 10 am to be operated on, as we heard this morning, for a perforated gastric ulcer. The system involves me in twice as much paperwork and Mollie half as much. Handy hates it, but has nothing to do with it. My desk is permanently littered with carbon paper as well as the usual ullage, and there are several new files around, in pretty pastel shades. The top of the stationery cupboard is now laid out for M's things only (I found myself explaining to the accountant yesterday which would be my first goals of sabotage when the imagined crisis occurs, and that that cupboard was very high on my list of priorities), and everybody is as happy as a fairy-tale king.

The table – isn't it the *end?* John [Hill] came in the shop and Handy showed him our need for another table, but I imagine very little will happen until a van actually carts it away. I thought I'd found a perfect substitute in a shop down the road [Chiltern Street] – a smashing oval walnut breakfast table – but dammit if it didn't happen to be 6" too long and therefore impossible. Mollie came here under sufferance . . . and the shop just happened to be shut for half an hour in the middle of the afternoon. She stalked up and down cursing me, the shop owner and the cold, then took a taxi back to vent her wrath . . .

Early in May I sent another fairy story about a witch who lived with her little slave Stand Aside. Mollie was then involved in the central garden of Barkston Gardens, Earls Court, and stories followed back to the shop of her problems with the committee. The story (too long to reproduce) told of the witch's rules for the garden which forbade anyone using it except the witch herself. A magician was summoned

31. Lady Violet Benson (see note 11 and letter of 31/5/68).

who turned the witch into a small cubicle "hung with red velvet curtains which had a green frieze", which was to be used exclusively by the local cats. The neighbours called it Buck's Folly.

H.H.   3/5/67

Betty Batten[32] . . . wants to ask you to dinner next Tuesday when I am going. She was going to write to the shop so I quickly switched her off that and gave her your address . . . One great good thing about dining with her is that she LIKES one to leave early . . . I am very fond of [Betty] but she is a bit of a boomer and one never knows what is coming next. Nancy [Mitford] and I call her Bluff King Hal.

Your last bulletin was as fascinating as ever. I still have not much time for response as children and grandchildren are down here. I will just add a few sayings which I found I had written down. Can you guess what famous man said them?

"I know that she has a comparatively high opinion of me from our telephone conversations.

The old chum's act.

By the length of a street.

My dear Fellow.

I could very nearly recite the whole of Sherlock Holmes to you.

Barley was a good man, you know. He was at Rugby in my time.

It isn't quite my cuppa.

It's damn near half time.

I told him he must be very ordinary and respectable if he works here. He can't look eccentric. I would have about ½ of his hair cut off."

---

32. Mrs Betty Batten, close friend of Heywood.

Perhaps you could add a few?

The Vyners are coming here for two nights on 16th. They will be sleeping where you slept so I promise to remove the plaque saying so and describing how you were bewitched.

H.H.   18/5/67

The Vs left this morning after their two nights here which I think passed quite successfully . . . We talked very little shop. There was a sort of mutual wariness (and weariness) about the subject . . . [Henry] asked if I had seen you lately and I said vaguely that we did meet you somewhere at dinner not long ago. He didn't ask where.

He has told Margaret that they MUST ask the Bs to dinner to stop them telling people that they (H & M) take no notice of them whatever. Margaret was not v. willing but agreed, so sent a postcard to Mollie and signed it "love, Margaret." Mollie took ten days to answer and then just signed it CMB. Do you think that Handy had fearful times getting her to go? . . .

I've been put in a fix by being sent a list of books which Mrs Mellon's daughter (living in Paris) wants. I am supposed to charge them to Mrs M's List – as written by her – is (I'll put it on a separate sheet in case you want to take it to the shop). I'll send a postcard to the shop asking if they will clique the Osbert Sitwell.[33] Can you help with any ideas about the Samuel Palmer and David Cox books? . . . I don't want to embroil you in my fixes and know that you must utterly keep out of it . . .

---

33. Walter Sickert, *A Free House*, edited by Osbert Sitwell.

J.S.S. 19/5/67

A very raw Friday, which included a double hammering from Handy and Mollie apropos some miserable cheque that I didn't put in its lawful place. Oh dear, these rules, and when you break them, the mangling and the mess. Of course I should have stepped down *prontissimo* and not been obstinate, because all the same old tosh came pouring out: "you don't understand any book-keeping and that's why . . ." and "what would happen if I started keeping a cheque in my drawer? . . ." Answer being that there wouldn't be any room there among his dirty books.

This Mellon business is awfully awkward . . .

You ask whether Handy might have had difficulty persuading Mollie to accept the Vyners' invitation. Yes, yes, and Rosemary [Clements; our current secretary] has in consequence heard the story of Mollie's life – *lucky* girl. M. said she couldn't possibly spend a whole evening with Henry V., all the old trouble would start up again, and Margaret would want to come and work in the shop. You see what I mean. I said they really ought to accept and that it could only do good for them all to meet. "Oh no, you don't understand . . . but I'll see what Handy says." And Handy got his way.

I'm delighted they're going, but goodness knows what they will find to talk about. Handy is a good deal less cocksure and dominating outside his own territory . . . Their temperaments look like oil and water: you could hardly conceive of two partners less party to each other's qualities . . .

H.H. 24/5/67

Many thanks for your letter and advice about books for Mrs M's daughter . . . I shall write to her . . . and tell her to write to the shop about them (not mentioning me). If only every body and every thing were not so loony, I could write to you direct to the shop and ask you to choose books for Mrs M each month and also get you to deal with her daughter direct. I am getting the Aldeburgh bookshop to send books to Mrs M occasionally and to bill her . . . I have to try to make a little extra money in order to live here, and, as the Bs won't let me be legal, I am forced into crime.

Betty Batten told me about her visit to the shop and how Liz would not let you get anywhere near her . . . I gave Betty a severe testing here last Sunday. The local paper advertised that the Aldeburgh Festival committee would be grateful if as many people as possible would come to the new concert hall at Snape so that the acoustics could be tested – with an audience. First of all the local paper got the day wrong so that the town crier had to be asked if he could cry the mistake in Aldeburgh (he refused because he had quarrelled with the Festival secretary – which, what with the Arabs and Israel as well,[34] goes to show that the shop is only the hopeless world in a nutshell – though perhaps a bit extra nutty). 800 people turned up at the Hall on Sunday afternoon including Betty and Anne and Lucy and me and what seemed to be the whole local population with their young. There was a very good commander-in-chief (I think from Decca) who said that what he wanted first of all was utter silence for three minutes (huge exit of babies in arms). That we achieved amazing well though Lucy said she nearly burst. Then he told us that the next test would be very dreadful and he gave us a sample of the piercing edgy screech which he said would have to go on at various intensities for a quarter of an hour (some of the cultured folk, who had come expecting to hear some exquisite Mozart, were seen to have tied scarves around their ears). He then said he was

---

34. The Six-Day War.

very sorry but now he was going to have to make three explo-
sions and that they were going to be appallingly loud and that
he advised us to block ears as tight as possible. He said that he
would count 1, 2, 3 and that 5 seconds afterwards the first
explosion would take place. The suspense was terrible. There
was a great deal of smoke but the bangs, though loud enough,
were not quite as awful as I had feared. When, after that, he
asked us to all stand up and to shout HELP in unison, we all
responded feelingly and vociferously. He asked us to do
that twice. There was then a breather, after which we were
allowed some pretty music. Betty behaved with greatest
courage though threatens to get her own back some time. We
agreed that we did not think we would have behaved so well
if Ben Britten and Peter Pears had not been standing near to
us. I have heard they were delighted by the result and that the
hall has been proved acoustically the finest in Europe. . . .

I shall probably have Margaret's account of the Vyner
dinner party. Sir Martyn and Lady Beckett[35] were to be there
as well as Mark Boxer and Lady Arabella Slice[36] – so that
could have made it higher grade for the Bs. . . .

J.S.S. 25/5/67

A splendid letter from you this morning that made me
laugh out loud. There surely won't be anything in the Festival
quite up to that rehearsal . . .

I sometimes long to know how much the customers have
been apprised of the set-up at no. 10. Mrs M's daughter must
think it very strange that some books come from Aldeburgh
but she's been encouraged to write to us for others, and what
of Mrs M. herself? I remember you saying that she didn't

---

35. Sir Martyn Beckett (1918–2001), architect.
36. Mark Boxer (1931–88), journalist and cartoonist, and Lady Arabella
Boxer (b. 1934), cookery writer.

really get on with Handy, but does she think that you retired on a saintly cloud?

Are you coming across nice things to sell to the shop or do you prefer your personal criminal underworld? Of course it is *mad* that we can't keep up an arrangement . . .

A great fog of silence descended on the Vyner dinner party from the time that the Bs finally accepted to go. Mollie seems to have been severely wigged by Handy and though she's spoken freely about her conversation with the Boxers, she never revealed that Henry and Margaret were the hosts. Handy has been silent; he was probably bored and sat like a dormouse all evening. Why should he make the effort when he is not among his worshippers and not on his own territory?

Meanwhile, I was having an extra-special birthday treat that same evening, being given dinner by Liz. Gasp. We had been given two tickets by Mrs Sacher[37] for any show we wanted to see, and we chose the Goldoni at the Aldwych. Liz had seen it before, of course, and did without her short-wave receiver,[38] but it was a v. jolly play and I enjoyed it. Proceedings afterwards were rather stilted. . . .

Although Heywood had not expected me to send a postcard from my holiday in Rome, a picture postcard, dated 6 June, survives, the subject of which "might be gravely misinterpreted if I'd sent it to the shop". It was the custom for anyone on holiday to send a series of postcards in strict order, first to Handy, then Liz, then the secretary and finally the packer. I told Heywood that Roman postcards were difficult to choose because they contained such wide possibilities of double-entendres and misunderstandings.

---

37. Mrs Michael Sacher (Audrey) (1917–84), loyal customer.
38. The receiver gave a simultaneous translation to those whose Italian was not fluent.

H.H.   29/6/67

I hope you were restored by your holiday and that it was not too grim getting back. By now it must be nearly time for the Bs' vacation – I cannot remember the dates. That'll be a hectic time for you – although with the compensation of head matron being absent.

Rumour may have reached you that I did ask the shop to send two books to Mrs M's daughter. I was surprised to get an acknowledgement this morning signed LOVE LIZ . . . I guess you found the most terrible pile of Cliquers[39] on your return. Anne and I have given up on our Alpine holiday. Can't leave her mother – as well as the Aldeburgh Festival being ruinous . . .

J.S.S.   2/7/67

The Bs are indeed away, until today fortnight. The shop will be terribly busy but please do come and look it up. There's no reason why Liz should take it amiss, but she might be glad of a smokescreen excuse to tell Mollie when they return: could you possibly pick up your type-writer from the packing room, or bring in a handful of children's books?

Sitwell's *A Free House* is meant to be on its way from Traylen,[40] as Handy had ticked the report and apparently dealt with it while I was away. During two weeks he managed to cope with ten books, two of which we didn't want. He's asked me to draw up a list of anything and everything that would come to my desk for the next time, and to treat him like a dotard (the humble Handy). He did not say *one word* about my holiday and Mollie's welcome home came as:

---

39. *The Clique*, weekly magazine in which second-hand booksellers advertised for wanted books.
40. A second-hand bookseller in Guildford.

"Your desk is absolutely disgusting, and you always leave drawers open. As for the time that you spend giving useless information to the customers, I cannot bear it any longer." She bore it another week and then went on holiday. . . .

Before leaving for Switzerland, Handy played a pretty cowardly trick by writing a raspberry to Henry that couldn't possibly be answered until his return. It consisted of four or five mean little complaints which Mollie had obviously been firing at him for weeks, but which he hadn't the courage to bring up at his fortnightly conferences.

[Some details followed about Rome and some of the people, including Muriel Spark, whom I'd met through my ex-uncle Ronald Bottrall.[41]]

H.H.   4/7/67

The shopcoming, after your holiday, seems to have followed the usual school pattern. Very disheartening. I rather long to hear what Handy's complaints were to Henry . . . If I do come I will commit no nuisance. I will only pick up my typewriter and sing the Liebestod to Liz (I don't believe even Liz could sneakily sing that back to darling Moll. Wish she would) . . .

J.S.S.   6/7/67

Tuesday next week would suit me best and I wonder if I could creep round to the Travellers and meet you for a drink. The story of Handy's letter has now gained momentum as I went to see Henry yesterday: it is going to lead to a Big Row, and Henry's going to be "very very tough". Full explanation when I see you.

---

41. Ronald Bottrall (1906–89), poet, whose first wife was my father's sister Margaret.

J.S.S. 24/7/67

I'm not sure I don't finish the day more shattered when Liz is on holiday than at any other time of the year. Handy takes ironical pleasure in comparing my own irritation at his incompetence with Liz's, and for three afternoons a week I have Mollie less than a yard away blazing about inaccuracies and worse. They're in fairly good heart at the moment because H. has sold a £27,000 book to Lady F[isher][42] – less than three hours after agreeing to buy it –, and M. has decided to spend some of her mother's legacy on some very classy carpet. But what, you may ask, of the Handy–Henry confrontation? To my chagrin I still don't know as I've heard nothing from Henry of what was said. Handy characteristically did nothing about replying to Henry's letter and let the whole thing lie until Henry moved. Henry was a bit baffled and rang me a week ago to ask what on earth was happening . . . Following my instructions, he demanded an immediate conference . . . The result cannot have been unfavourable from Handy's point of view, as he was particularly cheerful the next morning, assuring me that he was *impressed* by Henry's performance . . .

"Mr R. dealt ably in books in the same way that he would have dealt in tins of meat and other commodities – without knowledge or responsibility as to the proportion of rottenness or nourishment they might contain . . . He greeted D. with a crabbed goodwill and, putting on large silver spectacles, appeared at once to abstract himself in the daily accounts." From *Daniel Deronda*, which I read when I was in Italy: I specially like the tins of meat analogy as H. has often told me that he would have made a very successful butcher if he'd devoted himself to carcasses . . .

---

42. Lady Fisher was making a fine collection of great flower books.

H.H. 31/7/67

I enjoyed your bulletin v. much, and the quote from *Daniel Deronda* made me roar. It almost makes me want to try DD again; I believe that I tried years ago and stuck . . .

I hadn't dared to hope that there would be any satisfactory outcome of the LETTER episode. I guessed that Handy would be as dead dodgy as ever and would dodge out of it – using delaying tactics.

Anne and I had lunch with the Vs a fortnight ago in their new Sussex home [near Petworth]. Odd that it should be two miles away from my old home. When we arrived, I was appalled to see a fleet of cars outside the house, but they turned out to belong either to builders and decorators or to Henry – except for one which belonged to Billie Wallace[43] . . . Henry was looking, as often, like Ed[ward] VII the morning after and was not helped by a brilliant blue shirt with a huge white star pattern which hung over his trousers – American style. As soon as Billy had left, he burst out about Handy's letter and his answer to it, pathetically sure that he had at last got hold of some reins. He thought that his letter was going to be a bombshell. Probably Handy hardly bothered to read it . . .

I can remember the horror of Liz's holidays and Handy becoming Liz and prolonging of after-beer grumps . . . I believe that bigger and better carpets are darling Moll's whole aim in life.

You must come down here again after school hols are over. I wish it could be before but what with great gran [the Dowager Countess of Cranbrook, Anne's mother] being a great big kid herself and also with the return of an Edinburgh

---

43. Billie Wallace (1927–77), son of Mrs Barbara Agar, née Lutyens, and close friend of H.R.H. Princess Margaret.

tart and her half-black bastard as housekeepers, it's not poss. till then.

J.S.S.   2/8/67

Dead dodgy's just the word: Handy evaded the issue as slyly as you'd foreseen. He spiked Henry's guns in a couple of minutes: "Let's forget the unpleasantness of the letters we've exchanged, and I must humbly apologise for making a mistake of fact." No chance for Henry to put the blame on the invisible accountant, as Handy took full responsibility for everything. He'd been terribly tired when he'd written the letter, more than ready for a holiday. Yes, yes, said Henry, but while we're on this level, can we think positively about the future of the shop? Proposition (1) that it must go on making money, (2) that there must be someone trained to take over from Handy in x years time, despite his wanting, great man that he is, to see the shop collapse with him, and (3) that Henry himself must play a greater part in making decisions . . . In the last analysis Henry cares very much less for the shop than Handy. I had the feeling that he had almost dismissed the mishap from his mind once it had turned out a failure, and that he was irritated by the constant anti-B warfare carried on by Margaret and myself.

[The previous Friday, with Liz on holiday, I'd had a bad session with Mollie sitting opposite. The second of two accidents was the more memorable]. Mollie was talking to the accountants on the telephone. The formidable J[oan] Haslip[44] appears at the step flourishing a cheque and telling the assembled company that she is going to have no time to read *The Normans in the South*, and wants to bring it back;

---

44. Joan Haslip (1912–94), biographer (*The Lonely Empress, The Sultan*, etc.). She asked Handy to read and comment on her finished typescripts.

she has paid her bill minus £2.10 for *Normans*. Mutter mutter from Mollie as if she will lay an egg; she cannot get at Her Bills to extract the one written to Miss H. I am scribbling away at a label or something and am far too timid to put my hand into the tray of Her Bills. Her speech to the accountant gets faster and faster, and sweat breaks out on her peony forehead. Miss H. notices nothing. M's conversation at an end, she dives into her tray and finds the relevant bill. Yes, that is the right amount, thank you very much, and would you like a receipt? Miss H. leaves, and there's a pause of some seconds. Then "And why didn't you get out her bill from my tray as soon as she asked for it? Couldn't you see that I was having an important conversation about the accounts, and surely it wasn't difficult to find a bill? It doesn't surprise me that Handy says you're the worst mannered young man he's ever known." I blanch, and stammer out, "I very much hope you'll withdraw that." She left the shop within ten minutes, the rest of her afternoon's work left to me.

I spent a fairly unhappy evening alone, working out a speech or two to make to Handy next morning, none of which actually came to my lips at the operative moment: how is it possible to be rude about your boss's wife to the boss himself? I merely said that life was going to be a bit difficult if Mollie continued to say that sort of thing to me. "I suppose you don't realize," he replied, "how incredibly rude you are yourself, and that we all have to put up with a very great deal. Mollie speaks in this forthright way and I'm not sure it isn't the best way to deal with difficulties; she mastered Liz in a flash, and has had no trouble with her since. On the other hand, I have been if anything too patient, and I should perhaps have dealt with Liz harshly when she first came to work here. Do you know how you push past me and the customers without waiting until we get out of your way? Do you know how often you correct us all in your schoolmasterly way on little points of fact? And of course you must certainly develop a very much thicker skin as I can see at the moment that you are far too sensitive."

Well, to some extent I am impressionable, as this effusion wrecked me. I was glad to get away to the Lipscombs[45] for that afternoon and Sunday . . .

H.H.   11/8/67

I was talking to some women last week who, in the course of conversation, said that there is a recrudescence of witches in Devon and Somerset. I said stuff and nonsense and that I didn't believe in such superstition. However, one morning last week, I was sitting in bed reading your letter and Anne was sitting beside me sipping her tea when the handle of the tea cup broke off and the bed was flooded. Again – here I am writing to you – the window open on to an idyllic morning, sun twinkling on the dewy grass, when, suddenly, there is an appalling smell. I hear noises below and look out of the window to see an exposed man-hole with a plumber plumbing it.

If only Henry wasn't so feeble with his ducking stool. I have the same feeling as you that Henry doesn't enjoy anti-B talk. I suppose that he doesn't like it rubbed in – or to have to think – that he has such a hostile malevolent crew. It may also be right that he doesn't care much about anyone or anything. He is not imperceptive but he is still gullible by Handy. Who, after all, isn't?

You seem to have had a particularly gruesome end of July. I think that I must have spent half my life rehearsing speeches to the Bs which were never performed. It was not so bad for

---

45. John and Peg Lipscomb, my uncle and aunt, who lived in Chilham, near Canterbury, Kent.

me in that I could not be sacked – although there was constant danger of poison and plot. One of Lucrezia's charming methods of getting one's goat was saying vile things – always when there was no witness – about loved ones or favourite relations – Anne or Sheila or Jonny. As for Handy calling your voice schoolmasterly, if ever there was a schoolmaster's voice, it's HIS . . . Keep on with the bulletins. I am sure that it is good for you to let off occasional steam and only Anne and I can profoundly understand the true cause of the boiling. You ought to write a daily shop diary when you get home in the evenings. Think what fun you will have in publishing it in 2000 AD – or even earlier. That really would be the last laugh.

While writing this, a vet and a piano-tuner have called. My mother-in-law says that the vet is not the usual one who comes and that the piano-tuner has got so thin that she did not recognize him. Do you think that the plumber, the vet and the piano-tuner are all the same person and that that person left her broomstick at the gate?

J.S.S.   16/8/67

I've raised the idea in the shop that I might benefit by doing a catalogue of children's books – never of course suggesting that it would be to the shop's benefit, only to my own, educationally etc. – , but we've somehow mislaid the folder with all your old catalogues. Handy has naturally kept his own, but I cannot put my hands on the others and I'd like to see the appropriate style (size, print and fullness of detail) before I start. It couldn't be ambitious because the children's stock is relatively poor . . . but there may be a new market developing and I guess that it'll be very much more difficult to find good stock at reasonable prices within very few years . . .

I loved your witchery and have passed it on to Rosemary and Mr Stafford – a very good laugh all round, plus sympathy over the tea-soaked bedclothes. Let me know about further phenomena.

My contract was presenting further problems: "Handy inserted a clause that he reserved the right to sack me at his own discretion without reference to anyone else" – a clause which amazed my solicitor and even caused a frisson in Henry. I even asked the question why I should stay; surviving for another six years until Handy retired seemed hard to imagine.

The letter ended with an imagined battle-array of Handy's friends and fans gathered round the general (Handy)'s tent where the flag flies in Old Rugbeian colours. Commanders of battalions included Michael Stanley,[46] Lady Violet Benson, Lady Pamela Berry[47] and Michael Tree;[48] they were defending Philistia against a more sensitive army which protected Parnassus.

H.H.   30/8/67

Hooverings are going on in my room so I cannot get at your last letter . . . I THINK that you asked if I had any spare shop catalogues. I have got a few which I would lend you; would like them back as they are all that I have left. Before flight I was v. tempted to steal the bound collection, feeling that they were mostly my own work – apart from one catalogue by [Joe] Hone[49] and a FEW great descriptions of great

<hr>

46. Michael Stanley (1921–90), whose London house was 39 Charles Street. Handy often stayed at the Stanleys' house in Westmorland. His wife Fortune was a sister of Mrs John Raven.

47. Lady Pamela Berry (1914–82), hostess, whose husband Michael's family owned *The Daily Telegraph*.

48. Michael Tree (1921–99), elder son of Ronald Tree and Nancy Lancaster; married to Lady Anne, sister of the Duke of Devonshire.

49. Joseph Hone (b. 1937), novelist.

descriptions of great books by the Buck (as Jim [McKillop][50] used to call him). Thank you so much for sending *Broomsticks*. It gave me quite a quiver when I saw the title as I felt after my last letter that maybe I was being hoist with my own broomstick . . .

Just got into my room and found your letter. I do see that, if an editorial job turns up, you could not but jump at it. I would of course selfishly mind . . .

Oh dear, the defence of Parnassus. I cannot think of much of a muster. I wouldn't call Philistia's lot TOUGH, more in the tweed class. I admit they would put up a jolly good show and all that but am not so sure that they would not crumple under steady fire of strong cross-bowmen and women like Mr Stafford, Diana Dykes,[51] Caroline Medway,[52] Cara Lancaster[53] . . . I fear that Osbert Sitwell's and Victor Stiebel's[54] arrows would now only be verbal, but nonetheless they might put out the excessive gas on the other side. I shall give the whole matter more thought. Of course, it goes without saying that you will be expected to win the day by changing sides in mid battle.

J.S.S.   1/9/67

I'd thought that, come September [my contract was finally about to be signed] and a new era opening for me in the shop, I'd write a daily diary. Of course there's much to be said in its

---

50. Jim McKillop, the shop's packer in the forties and fifties.
51. Diana Dykes, daughter of the Buchanans' solicitor; she worked in the shop for several years in the early sixties.
52. Caroline (née Jarvis), now the Countess of Cranbrook.
53. Cara, daughter of Osbert Lancaster (1908–86), cartoonist. Both she and Caroline Medway had worked at Heywood Hill.
54. Victor Stiebel (1907–76), couturier. After the *Evening Standard* interview with Handy Buchanan, he wrote him a scorching letter in support of Heywood.

favour but I don't want it to become a chore and there are many evenings when I'm too knackered to think, let alone recall. There would have been a jolly entry today if I didn't mind name-dropping: Angus Ogilvy[55] sheltering from the rain (before being picked up by his wife), and finding himself with Lanning Roper,[56] who in turn bearded Hugh Chisholm[57] (I've never been able to take the latter seriously since hearing Ronald Bottrall's story about him: HC was asking some favour in that smooth sub-English voice on the telephone, and RB asked him his name. HC said "Chisholm" very quietly as if everyone ought to know; when asked how to spell it, he said "Oh, the usual way"; RB countered "I wasn't sure if it wasn't C-H-I-zee-zee-U-M." Fury at the other end).

. . . If the contract [now re-drafted] goes through, I'm unlikely to leave in the next five years. Some of this will be very hard labour, but a good job in publishing doesn't grow on trees, and I will have to be patient. At the moment, I have more responsibility than is normal for someone of my age and the responsibility can only grow . . .

Autumn holidays are almost on us: Rosemary's on her much-envied 3-week jaunt in Sicily, Handy's off to Witherslack[58] in the middle of next week, and I'm planning a visit to Dublin for the last week of the month, because two friends[59] are marrying there on the 23rd . . .

---

55. Hon. Angus Ogilvy (1928–2005), businessman and husband of H.R.H. Princess Alexandra.
56. Lanning Roper (1912–83), gardener and writer.
57. Hugh Chisholm, well-read Anglophile American.
58. The country home of Michael and Fortune Stanley.
59. Alan Howarth (see note 7) was marrying Gillian Chance. The wedding was attended by Field-Marshal Montgomery.

H.H.   9/9/67

. . . I have just had Osbert Sitwell's yearly request to find him a Christmas present for the Queen Mother. I have got a little book here called *Chapters on Coronations*, 1838, which may possibly do though it's not much to look at. I shall tell him about it . . .

There has been an Antique Dealers Fair going on in the concert hall here during the past few days. Quite a lot of dealers from London and all v. pretentious and expensive. One bookseller from Ipswich. I looked at a set of Gibbon – mid 19th century, bound in school vellum: £50. After that I gave up.

J.S.S.   17/9/67

. . . A very nasty moment on Friday afternoon, when I had to admit to Mollie that I'd signed my side of the contract, without Handy having approved the final draft. "I should have thought that reason enough to have sacked you on the spot," she said and, a little later, "Why is it, John, that you always prefer to trust anyone but Handy?" She then slinked (slunk!) down to the print room while I looked after the shop alone, my nerves exposed to all and every element and she made a couple of telephone calls – to whom? Whatever she heard must have reassured her because there was no more nagging – saving her fire for Handy's return from Westmorland that evening. She must have laid into him fair and square because his post-holiday chatter next morning – my goodness, he can be boring – ended fairly abruptly when I'd done the receipts, and he said "What about this contract then?" in a tone that suggested he'd been through pros and cons for hours. I explained satisfactorily and was told for the umpteenth time how long he'd waited for his own contract and what a blackguard Henry had always been . . .

Do you remember a pamphlet hidden away in one of the cupboards called *Horrors of Slavery*? I was stocktaking a fortnight ago and thought it worth reporting to James Pope-Hennessy[60] whose new book, *Sins of the Fathers*, is about the Atlantic slave trade. He seems v. pleased to have it and he's invited me for a drink tomorrow evening; I shall need to be circumspect about his book which I found too scissors-and-pastey . . .

Could I invite myself for the first weekend in November – ages ahead, but before Gethsemane and therefore negotiable? And if you're coming to London before then, I've got a few books like the first vol. of [Michael Holroyd's] *Lytton Strachey* and the new Angus Wilson[61] . . .

H.H. 6/10/67

Brilliant that you found *School Inspector*;[62] I never thought it possible. It will do splendidly as a birthday present for Anne. I'm v. grateful too for *L. Strachey* which I have just begun and see I am going to find completely absorbing . . .

H.H. 23/10/67

Yesterday my mother-in-law fell and broke her hip and had to be taken into a hospital in Ipswich to have that pinning-up operation. Anne has just come back from being with her all day and says that so far she appears to have got through it wonderfully well. They say that she will have to be there for probably quite a month, [but this] shouldn't interfere with your weekend of Nov. 3rd, which we are looking forward to . . .

---

60. James Pope-Hennessy (1916–74), biographer of Queen Mary and others; also a colourful shop customer.
61. The new novel was *No Laughing Matter*.
62. A. J. Swinburne, *Memories of a School Inspector*, c. 1910.

Holland [where they had spent a week's holiday] was a great success and we even survived the gale force 9 which we plunged back through . . . Of course, I didn't have time to read much of Lytton S. though I'm now ½ of the way through. I can see that I shall end by buying a copy as yours has slightly suffered from its voyaging and, also, Anne MUST read it. I continute to be fascinated though sometimes wonder how right the author's rather dogmatic judgements always are . . . I admire and enjoy the book very much and can't wait for Vol. 2 where I shall have known far more of the people. I once had dinner alone with Lytton in his flat (Gordon Square I believe) and I remember it was hilarious and I liked him immensely. He didn't make a pass and I don't believe that I suspected that was why he had asked me. Probably however that is very conceited and that I was a grave disappointment. I remember us shrieking with laughter at some bust of him that had just been done . . .

J.S.S.   25/10/67

. . . Very sorry to hear about your ma-in-law's hip . . . It's rather awful for you to be hospital visiting in Ipswich for a month, but better that than regular trips to the grand Hip Centre near Wigan to which some of the customers have had to repair . . .

Henry had me to lunch at Brooks's last Wed. – he specifically preferred it to White's because there are so many HH customers around at White's. The usual crowd was there: G[eoffrey] Gilmour,[63] G[eorge] Harwood,[64] Sir J[ock]

---

63. Geoffrey Gilmour (d. 1981), collector and friend of Nancy Mitford in Paris.
64. George Harwood (1908–85), businessman and bibliophile. I once mistook him for Mr Nubar Gulbenkian, which immensely pleased him.

Balfour[65] and the ubiquitous R[oger] Longrigg.[66] We had a pretty filthy lunch but caught up on shop business without too many people overhearing. On Thursday Handy had a date for lunch with Derek Priestley.[67] Where did they go but Brooks's and he came chuntling back with stories of how many shop customers he had seen: John Evelyn,[68] G. Harwood and the ubiquitous R. Longrigg; no stories of the lunch, it was enough that he had been seen lunching at a Club. No word of the near-coincidence has filtered back to the shop, and it doesn't really worry me if it does: why *shouldn't* Henry give me lunch from time to time . . .?

My second weekend in Snape passed with less incident than the first, but I left behind the catalogue for the current Turner exhibition. Heywood returned it, enclosing a letter, now lost, and the GPO charged me postage due. An umbrella "past caring for", but also left, could be "swapped one day for the doll's house." My Collins to Anne was undated. Heywood had offered a few books for me to buy for shop stock. When I asked Handy to draw a cheque for £10, "he supposed that the shop could just afford my spending as much as that on mistakes, because after all I had to learn". The following day, "to my delight Mrs Black came in at lunchtime and bought nearly £8 worth of the very same books . . . a Minor Triumph for Our Side".

---

65. Sir John Balfour (1894–1983), diplomat.
66. Roger Longrigg (1929–2000), novelist under his own name and others.
67. Derek Priestley (1912–2000), managing director of Peter Davies, publishers, part of the Heinemann Group, with offices near Heywood Hill.
68. John Evelyn (1904–76), eccentric, poet and descendant of the famous diarist. He lived at 33 Grosvenor Square and was one of the shop's best customers.

J.S.S. [7/11/67]

I cannot disbelieve in witchcraft, in spite of its tricks being less apparent during the weekend. The effects were postponed until yesterday evening when I was out to dinner and had to refuse to eat and drink because I felt so green ... [the sickness] went away as quickly as it arrived: I survived today without any hint of queasiness or qualm ...

J.S.S. 13/11/67

I seem to have been sating myself with *Lytton Strachey* ... [criticism follows on the same lines as Heywood's, but I didn't want to put him off reading the second volume "because so much of L. S. *sans* Holroyd is so fascinating"].

Have you solved Sir O. Sitwell's Christmas present this year? Is it worth my suggesting *Deliciae Britannicae* which you bought some time ago? Like a fool I've left the bibliographical details on a pad in the shop, but you may remember it's about three royal palaces, Windsor, Hampton Court and Kensington, date c. 1730, with about 8 engravings, price £7.10. If it sounds promising, I'll report it properly and you could write in full to our anti-Philistine ally.

Nancy [Mitford] appeared at 5.20 p.m. today but she will be able to give you a better account than me: I stay mum.

H.H. 22/11/67

How vile of the post office to penetrate my parcel. I suppose they find those porridge paddibags so easy to penetrate.

I had been waiting to answer you until Nancy had been over here last weekend – hoping she would sparkle with shop gems which I could flash back to you, but I never saw her alone and she was so busy chatter boxing with Cynthia

Gladwyn[69] that she hardly mentioned the place – except to say that she had "lived" there last week and that Handy had been annoyed when she told him that, when people asked how they could look at *Chips*[70] without buying it, she told them that they should go to the shop and do their peeping standing at a table. Actually, we never do let much hair down between us . . . partly, I think, because she has changed sides twice and also because she was once such friends with Mollie . . .

I have nearly finished ploughing through ELEANOR OF AQUITAINE (not the new book [by Régine Pernoud] – one published in the 50s). At first it made me think that people were even more beastly to one another in those times – but I believe that it was really only in less subtle ways – like chopping off hands and gouging out eyes.

J.S.S.   27/11/67

. . . not at all surprised that Nancy didn't come up with treasures; she didn't really get much chance, everyone was on such model behaviour . . . I'd rather looked forward to the meeting, long prepared, between N. and Mollie . . . M. appeared from behind her screen blushing as I've never seen her – the Red Queen before her Maker. They then sat down again tête à tête, with Handy dancing attendance like a puppet footman. For this he earned what he would call a wigging, for talking all the time while M. was dying to have a good gossip with N. by herself. I'd never realized the extent to which Mollie has imitated and affected Nancy-esque mannerisms: it was quite worrying not to be able to tell their higher

---

69. Lady Gladwyn (1898–1990), née Noble, wife of Gladwyn Jebb, diplomat.
70. Robert Rhodes James's edition of Chips Channon's diaries.

pitched laughs apart. And how amazing that N. doesn't hate the affectation: she was charm herself, with tongue never once in cheek. She mentioned that she had been in Suffolk and had seen you in Snape, and I can only remember Mollie saying that you had always loved doing nothing . . .

A pity you couldn't come into the shop this afternoon. Handy bought a set of Redouté *Lilies* and sold it for £5000 to Lady F. within two or three hours; Liz had George Cukor's[71] Christmas list and her hero for ½ hour and I kept everyone else at bay and mysteriously managed to tread on important corns. Not that I interrupted either major business, but Handy glowered for the rest of the afternoon and is clearly harbouring a grievance . . .

H.H. 7/12/67

Your description of the Red Queen before her Maker was fascinating. I suppose that some of the expressions like QUEEN MUM, and people such as Lady Vi being POPPETS and SWEETIE-PIES, have become archaic and that the R.Q., always attuned to the upper-class with-it swing, may have moved on to other forms . . . Nancy is very swayable and it is quite possible that, by underhand methods, she could be swayed back into the other camp. But she is loyal – so will probably stick to both sides. A great debunker was lost in Malcolm Bullock[72] who used to taunt her with Mollie's passion for her and postcards like "If Mollie leaves, so do I."

I fear that your worstest hour of agony and bloody sweat is upon you . . .

71. George Cukor (1899–1983), film director.
72. Sir Malcolm Bullock (1890–1966), diplomat.

J.S.S. 24/12/67
[Christmas Eve, "a most unsatisfactory day"]

Brian Howard, Portrait of a Failure[73] was delivered to the shop on Friday. Handy let me have [this advance copy] with extreme reluctance, only on condition that I posted it back as soon as I had finished. This I have done and, my goodness, what a brilliant book it has become: I have written a note to Mrs Lancaster to congratulate her on the editing . . . Of course there will be plenty of people in the enemy camp who will say B.H. isn't worthy of a 600 page biography. That I should have enjoyed it so much results partly from my knowledge of the shop and my experience of your inheritance. I would have been blindly uncomprehending about such a man and such a life three years ago . . .

[A page has disappeared here; it must have referred to Mollie's rebuking me again for not shutting my desk drawer.] The trouble is, as I said to Mr Stafford, that Mollie has never been able to open her drawers: many of her problems would have been meaningless if she hadn't kept them tightly closed.

There was plenty [in the two weeks before Christmas] that was rewarding: unexpected meetings between customers, a visit from Jean Shrimpton[74] who signed her cheque to Hatchards and apologized when I had caught her up in the street, and about £10,000 worth of trade, including an unprecedented £1200 or so in ready cash. We wonder if our casual trade [i.e. non-account customers] has increased since Bumpus and Burton[75] have both disappeared. The work was devastating.

---

73. The composite biography, edited by Marie-Jaqueline Lancaster, was to be published by Anthony Blond. It was reprinted in paperback in 2005.
74. Jean Shrimpton (b. 1942), model, then living in Albany with Terence Stamp.
75. Bumpus in Mount Street and Burton in Berkeley Street, booksellers within easy walking distance, had closed in the previous twelve months.

1968

. . . I suppose that by now you have had your convalescent week. I hope that you are restored . . . I was interested that you had enjoyed *Portrait of a Failure*; I had wondered how it would hit someone who had not known Brian. I only read a very rough draft of it – before it had been "pulled together".

Did I tell you that I had got involved in talking (among a lot of others) on the wireless about it? I don't expect I did because didn't want anyone to listen and was certain it would mean emigration. I bet it got winded among the Philistines.

I managed to get Eddie[76] roped in too, who knew Brian better than I did. It was a triumph to have got him to do it. He said he only would if they would record him down here. I thought that would let us off – but it didn't . . . When the engineer arrived, I had to go with him and Pocock [the producer] into our sitting room where an awful microphone had been erected on the table. I started off – thinking to myself that I was sounding like the Queen on Christmas Day – when, suddenly, the engineer said STOP – THERE IS A HUMMING NOISE. None of us could quite trace it, but we thought it to be the washer-up which we switched off (After they had gone, Anne and I discovered that it had been the night-storage heater). That was disconcerting . . . I did once refer to "my bookshop". That will cause a tremendous odour, what? They absolutely mutilated Eddie's [contribution] which had been extremely amusing. As I feared, they cut out two lines of Brian which he quoted (lines from a rhymed commentary which B. wrote after he and Eddie had been bored by some

---

76. Hon. Edward Gathorne-Hardy (1901–78), Anne Hill's second brother.

mutual acquaintance giving them a tedious description of a so-called love affair):–

He heaves a sigh and then undoes a button;
Can it be love or just a glutton's mutton?

[Much discussion of *Lytton Strachey*, vol. 2] . . . It will be dreadfully easy for mockers to pick on. All those tangled relationships can so easily be made to be thought ludicrous . . . but what art it takes to avoid the ludicrous in describing almost ANYONE's intimate life. It's strange – perhaps admirable – that so many beans should have been spilled by the survivors. Of the two I knew well, Ralph and Frances Partridge,[77] it gives a wrong idea of Ralph. It seems to make him out difficult and hysterical, where he was an absolute rock and pillar to a great many people, and altogether a unique and splendid character. Had a wonderful way of talking. Was brilliant at doing nothing and enjoying it (could make enough to live on by looking at a newspaper).

Here I was interrupted and I must anyway stop gassing, especially knowing how much gas and gaiters you have to endure. I am thinking of sending a brief note to Handy offering him a copy of Norman Douglas's *Experiments* which Eddie wants to sell. It's one of the original signed limited (300) copies; inscribed to Eddie from Eddy Sackville-West(the other way round I've just discovered, with Eddy S.W.'s bookplate).[78] I imagine it ought to be worth about £15 – or do you think more – or less. Privately Printed, 1925. I'd quite like to give H. one more chance of answer – and then, if he doesn't this time, give up for ever.

If only L. Strachey had lived to write EMINENT SHOP-WALKERS. The mantle may fall on you – you never know.

---

77. Ralph Partridge and his wife Frances, née Marshall (1900–2004), Bloomsbury diarist.
78. Hon. Edward Sackville-West (1901–65), novelist and essayist.

J.S.S.   3/2/68

A morning to myself at [my parents'] home for once . . . I haven't had time off like this since my week after Christmas, and already I could do with another break, so busy (& prosperous) has January been.

I missed the Brian Howard programme a second time as I had a dinner out that evening and I couldn't persuade the assembled company to tune in . . . many [customers] have expected us to know about it and of course we should.

There's a conversation which has repeated itself many times in the last three weeks. It runs like this:

X. Who was Brian Howard? (Pause, looks at back of dustwrapper). Oh yes, failure, yes, I suppose you must have known him well?

Handy: Knew him only too well, used to come here day after day, very close friend of Heywood Hill's.

X. What's the book like then, pretty heavy?

H. Yes, far too much written, and *terribly* expensive; should have been half the price. It obviously reads better if you didn't know Brian: John enjoyed it (ushering me into the conversation), he can tell you more about it.

J. I thought it was a very clever bit of editing and of course it's a fascinating piece of the literary scene etc. etc.

X has been put off the book already: he may have prejudices against Brian-types already, but Handy has confirmed him in his Good Sense. Liz is much more forthright: "simply can't take it".

We had a splendid "encounter" a week ago, suitable for *Eminent Shopwalkers*: the protagonists Captain [Ali] Mackintosh,[79] tottering and to all intents and purposes dead on his

---

79. A clubman whose memoirs, *No Alibi*, had been published in 1961.

feet, and Sherman Stonor,[80] rather the better for his lunch at the St James's [Club].

CM. Anything for me today?

SS. (from the other side of the front table without a word of introduction) I can very much recommend a book here on James I: it's dedicated to my wife and myself, and written by Archbishop Mathew[81] who . . .

CM. He's the old fairy

SS. . . . acts as my private Chaplain. He's done years of research into the subject and it's a really good biography . . . (Ready to expand for hours)

CM. Yes, I'd like that, I'll take that (and exit).

Did you ever get letters from Major Abbey?[82] One has been sitting on Handy's desk [written from the West Indies] this week, and I cannot get over his total illiteracy: he has been reading "Nickison's Diaries", and thinks "McMillan" might be too tough, and wonders whether there might be any "Memoirs or Autobiographies in Papper Back". John Roland Abbey, bibliophile, *illa scripsit*.

Muriel Spark [who had corresponded with me since our meeting in Rome] has asked what books have been published in the autumn. I'd told her some of the things we'd sold well, including the biography [by Fawn Brodie] of Sir Richard Burton. Her reply was very merry and included a paragraph that went "Who was Sir Richard Burton? If I show shocking ignorance, you should be able to earn some money from Texas University"[83] . . . I may have gone too far when describing Isabel Burton as a "ghastly Roman Candle prig".

---

80. Hon. Sherman Stonor (1913–76) later Lord Camoys, of Stonor Park, Henley-on-Thames.

81. David Mathew (1907–75), historian.

82. J. R. Abbey (1894–1969), distinguished book-collector. He had been reading Harolds Nicolson and Macmillan.

83. Texas was the major buyer of English literary manuscripts.

Henry gave me lunch at the Washington [Hotel] on Thursday, to tell me about his grand coup for Marlborough R[are] B[ooks]. They have just bought the cream of the Warwick Castle Library for an enormous sum under the very nose of Christie's. A thousand books or so, wonderful stock for three or four years: Henry was jubilant.

Could I come to Snape in the Spring? It's such a treat to get away from the Stink.

H.H. 2/2/68

. . . With immense labour I packed up Eddie's copy of N. Douglas's *Experiments* and sent it off to Handy a week ago. Dead silence, of course (I asked him to send Eddie a cheque for whatever he thought reasonable). Not that I expected there could be an answer before a month but it would be kind, if you happen to notice the book bending under a pyramid (it is in its original boards and therefore delicate) if you could without being detected, move it up to nearer the surface.

Anne and I went innocently to that film called Bonnie and Clyde last night not knowing what it was about and half expecting some sweet love story. We came away shattered by pouring blood and people's heads blown off . . .

J.S.S. 5/2/68

. . . It's disgraceful of Handy in every way – rude, careless but, I guess, deliberate. *Experiments* was very visible on his desk for a couple of days, and he asked for my confirmation on his offer: he thought he should give £15. I asked pretty pointedly on two occasions whether we had yet bought it, and I guardedly repeated the question this afternoon, but can I prod him into action? Apparently not . . .

H.H. 10/2/68

. . . I ought to have known better than to have tried *Experiments* with Handy. I shan't try any more . . . but only if I find some sacred Thornton[84] – something he really wants, which isn't likely. . . . Eddie of course wants the cash.

I'm not surprised by shop reaction to the B. Howard book – exactly what I'd have predicted. I had dinner with Betty Batten one night last week who was also pretty boring about it tho' she had to admit that she couldn't stop reading it. Once Brian delighted Betty by calling her DULCE DOMUM but, the next time, as was his wont, he went and ruined everything by shouting MURDERESS at her, just after her first husband had been shot down in an aeroplane.

Anne has finished the Lytton book. We had some fascinating talks about it all with Frances Partridge who stayed here last weekend. She showed us a marvellous but awful 30 page letter from Gerald Brenan[85] written while spending nights sitting with his dying wife . . .

I note from an advert in the Times Sat. Rev. that Rosicrucians know how to impress their personality on others to better their business and social position. Do you think that may be the secret of the Bs' success? Had we better endeavour to become SCRIBES?[86]

H.H. 18/2/68

Could you be v. kind and some time put on a postcard R. Vanderbilt's address.[87] He sent me a fan postcard about my broadcast but didn't write the address.

---

84. Thornton's *Temple of Flora*.
85. Gerald Brenan (1894–1987), travel writer and Hispanophile.
86. Scribes are, presumably, Rosicrucian disciples.
87. Robert Vanderbilt (b. 1918), who had owned and run the Holliday bookshop in New York from 1951 to 1961.

It was an extraordinary letter marked PERSONAL which you kindly forwarded. It was from somebody I was with at Eton and who had read the B. Howard book and was asking if I was the same Hill. He had spent long years in the Grenadier Guards but was never much good at bayonet fighting. He had been to Eton, Oxford, Cambridge (yes, both it seems), Sandhurst, but had only learnt the colour of Ovid's wife's hair. "Owing to a gigantic sacking in the house of Homosextualists [his spelling] I suddenly found myself Senior Wet Bob." Later he adds that he is going to "write lots".

Looking into a box yesterday I found an envelope marked "Horrible shop Letters". Some of them may amuse you when you next come down.

J.S.S. 19/2/68

I had a lucky break in Cambridge on Saturday and found a little nest of 1820-ish chap-books which had only been in David's[88] for an hour when I dropped in. Three of them I took to the shop this morning and they were duly approved: I even managed to pay myself back, so the fourth doesn't need to make any big money. But it is rather special and I've kept it back in case it might do for Mrs Mellon . . . Its wrapper reads: WONDERS! Description of some of the Most Remarkable of Nature and Art. St Michael's Volcano, Pyramids and Sphinx, Giant's Causeway . . . (12 others) Printed for J. Harris and Son, Corner of St. Paul's Churchyard. Date 1821 . . . Could you report it to her for £6 or £7 . . . as long as you can also make a profit? . . .

Not much gossip around. We sold nearly 60 copies of Lytton Vol. 2 pre-publication, and, at 84/- a smack, Handy couldn't complain of turnover. We actually broke our record

---

88. G. David, second-hand booksellers, with a shop off King's Parade.

for February by the middle of the month. H. had sold Furber's *Calendar of Fruit* for £1000 to Lady F., and a brilliant 4 volume shell book, Martin's *Universal Conchologist*, for £1400 to Fortune [Stanley] . . . One might hope for a little warmth to filter through the old brute's veins. Instead, he took the chance when Mollie was away, "to smarten me up": a process that I need hardly describe, consisting as it always does of a catalogue of his own virtues.

H.H.   22/2/68

Alas, WONDERS is one of those which I sold to Mrs M[ellon] . . . I believe that, deep in a file, I have my original description but today I am too rusted to start delving because of having spent hours composing a letter to my aunt who had written to me enclosing a letter to her from my Australian cousin, which said "Have morals disappeared in England now? Would you think it strange if a young girl stayed with a man alone in her flat? Is this generally accepted? I want to know what you think. Out here we still disapprove of such things." I've written her an enlightened sermon which I hope she will forward to Australia. It's a masterpiece though it will probably mean I shall be disinherited (of no great fortune, however; not even the quarter of a Furber) . . .

I have just managed to sell to Mrs M some original water-colours of Kate Greenaway. They also belonged to Eddie but, unlike *Experiments*, this time I charged a commission . . .

H.H.   14/3/68

Anne and I have been away for a fortnight on a little round of visits and only got back yesterday . . . We found A's mother fairly ill, some sort of bronchial thing. A's other brother, Antony, is now here as well as Eddie because his wife Ruth is in hospital. Don't tell the witches that this place is now a nursing home as nothing would delight them more. I myself have been attacked by some savage form of rheumatism but hope that will evaporate before too long. All the sympathy I get from Eddie is "Result of VD in your youth, I suppose, my dear."

We enjoyed our round. Ended up at Long Crichel[89] where Desmond Shawe-Taylor played me old records – including "A Fairy went a' Marketing", sung by Clara Butt. Super . . .

J.S.S. 15/3/68

. . . Handy retired to bed with a cold in mid-week, and I was left to the mercy of the Women on Wed. – no more than usually unpleasant, but still dismaying when you never find it improves. But this is *nothing* compared to your troubles. . . . I wonder whether you'd like a proof of *Somerville and Ross* by Maurice Collis; very light and Irishly funny.

Did you see our name (mis-spelt) in the Times on Tues. morning in their report of Monday's sale? Goodness knows why, in a fiendishly expensive sale otherwise, they should have remarked on the price we paid (£16) for a beautiful *Zuleika Dobson* . . . Muriel Spark [who had started collecting Beerbohm first editions] hasn't yet dabbled in really high stakes like this; I'm not good at persuading customers to buy books, at least by letter, that I could never afford myself (in the £70 to £100 bracket) . . .

With the above I included an account of a memorable
incident that same afternoon. I called it TRADE, a true story.

---

89. Long Crichel House in Dorset, shared by Desmond Shawe-Taylor, Raymond Mortimer and Eddy Sackville-West. Patrick Trevor-Roper and Derek Hill were involved later.

X walks into 10 Curzon St in mid-afternoon – in Handy's terminology, respectable; age around 40. A minute later I see he is carrying Strachey Vol. 2 in his newspaper, not trying to conceal it, but a Vol. 2 is missing from the pile on the middle table and Hemingway's Selected Journalism, its next door neighbour, pushed (accidentally?) on top. He turns to me and asks if he can look at children's books. Yes, of course, I say, downstairs; I'll follow you down; introduce you to the girl, who knows all about books for children.

On getting downstairs, he says that in fact he wants about 120 books, perhaps more. My face falls and he explains that they are to be sent to a school in Africa: rather retarded-for-reading children of 8 to 14. "Well" I say, "I'm not sure we can very easily do this, as we're in no way experienced about educational books, and the selection that is in the shop might not cover all categories; wouldn't it be better to look first at somewhere like the Children's Book Centre in Kensington Church St., where there will be a very much wider range?" [Sorry this all sounds terribly ordinary but the detail is important; as yet there's nothing of the slightest suspectness]. "No, no," he replies, "I find Kensington too boring, and Church St. is a part I don't like at all. Perhaps I should add that the books are to go out in twenties, so that I only want you to find seven or eight suitable books." Rosemary and I then look happier and with some patience we produce enough books to satisfy – well illustrated and thin enough to pack easily for posting. We metaphorically rub our hands, as he's thus far ordered between £150 and £200. He has appeared to know very little about children's books, educational or otherwise, and his choice is pretty random. Then comes the question of money:–

J. (rather quaking) I wonder as we're ordering such a collection of books, whether you could give us some guarantee . . .

X. Of course I understand (not very confidently). Perhaps you would like to add up the figures now and I'll pay you a cheque; or could I send you one for £50 in the post tomorrow morning?

J. No, no, we haven't got all the books and it'll really be too difficult to pay now, but we would be most grateful for some sort of er-um deposit.

X. Good, then we can leave that, but I must give you my name and address so that you can contact me about the atlas that you're ordering.

He gives us the following: Breadalbane and Holland, Embley Park, Liphook, Hants. No clue about his own identity. Then:–

X. There's just one other favour I'd like to ask of you (he moves towards the Strachey in his newspaper). There's been some confusion between my wife and me about buying this book, and I hope you may be able to take it back (oh yes, I mutter), and give me money in exchange. My wife bought it for cash here last week and in view of this very big order I wonder if you could help me. (Things are really racing through my mind now. Could I have made a mistake about the Strachey pile upstairs? Could I possibly face Mollie with the story that I had to refund a man (total stranger, was he, John? How *could* you?) – four guineas? And on the other hand could I risk losing £200 worth of business simply on a petty principle?)

So I hedge, and he becomes more insistent, and somehow to my eyes and ears the story doesn't wash: hoping to run up £200 credit on a firm's name in Hampshire and then asking for cash down on an inconspicuous exchange. So, agony of agony, with Rosemary listening to every word from her desk and cringeing, I have tentatively but definitely to accuse him of bringing the book down from upstairs. My manner must have been that of an idiot, as I cannot remember my being able to produce a single coherent sentence.

He denied it, as he was bound to, and agreed if I felt this way that the Strachey should be credited, and set against the pile of children's books. He then left, thanking us both profusely for the trouble we had taken.

A narrative leaves a lot of it out, and it's difficult to give X a more definable character. Perhaps one of the problems was that he was naturally undefinable; it would not surprise me if he wasn't touched and that, like Mr Loveday, he meant to enjoy his little outing. We shall *see*. If a cheque arrives, well and good; if he's prepared to come next week and approve the school atlas, fine. But I wish he hadn't made an hour of this afternoon such absolute torture.

My confidence was partially restored by a nice Belgian couple who wanted to start an account and who rejoiced under the name of PEKELHERING.

H.H.   17/3/68

I should love to borrow the Somerville and Ross proof if you can really spare it . . . Anne's mother is astonishingly better though we still live in a muddle of nurses and commodes.

H.H.   25/3/68

You may have heard via the desk that Anne's mother died last week – so I haven't been able to write, as you can imagine: a great many things, and people, to be dealt with. It has been sad during the last two years to watch her health failing and to see her becoming so much less the splendid person she used to be. I mean like when, during the War, she drove a pony and trap into Saxmundham to put some money into the Bank. When she got there, the pony began to buck and she put the money under her foot while she held his head but forgot about them and they all blew away . . . I remember a dog eating her false teeth and, another day, a mouse running across her bed and getting drowned in the po.

Somerville and R. and also your splendid true story were the best things that you could have sent to cheer one up during this sad period . . . As far as [the latter], I was of course fascinated and almost broke out in a rash myself. I long to know the sequel. . . . Do you remember that extraordinary American woman called Tiger something, who I got when I was alone one Saturday morning. She collected a pile of the oddest oddments like A History of Noses and she was so eccentric that I decided to trust her when she said she would send a cheque (& was staying at Carlton Towers) – though, when I watched her out of the window climbing into a racing car with some cad and both of them bursting with laughter, I guessed I'd been done. There were some nasty desk innuendoes after that . . .

J.S.S.   27/3/68

Trade has developed amazingly, you will hardly believe the final coincidence. On Friday morning Rosemary discovered that the shop cheque-book had disappeared – *calamitas calamitatum,* just imagine – , and we pinned the crime rightly or wrongly on to Mr X. This seemed to me premature and a bit hysterical, but we obviously had to stop cheques then and there. I became much more suspicious when I found from telephone directories in the PO that X had invented the name of his firm, his address and telephone number. Even this wasn't conclusive, as he would have had to rifle the drawer in less than a minute, when Rosemary leapt up the stairs to ask me a question. The bank got in touch with us this morning and said that the cheque-book had been used in three differ-ent shops, among them Austin Reed, which had accepted a cheque for £22, signed by B. Heywood. So we got in touch with the police, and I was interviewed by two very junior offi-cers this afternoon: my story has become pretty fluent since Thursday, and they seemed satisfied. I left the shop a little early because a terrible hang-over from last night + usual Wednesday-ana had reduced me to pulp, and came straight back to the flat. At 5.30 X was outside a shop-window in Chiltern St in an Austin Reed lightweight jacket. Could I arrest him? Should I have played the ignorant tradesman and reminded him of the various books we had ordered for him? I rang the Savile Row police station and, after two or three minutes, got through to the Petty Crimes Officer: he advised me to order a car straight along from Scotland Yard. Well, I may be a fool sometimes but I wasn't going to ring for a car only to discover that the man has disappeared in the mean-time. By the time I'd talked to Savile Row, X had disappeared. (I ran down to Blandford St, but there wasn't a sign.) O God, the frustration, with no way of following him up. [But] his face has now been pigeon-holed in my mind so that nothing will erase it.

What a con. When I first wrote on Thurs. evening, I felt guilty that I might have accused X falsely. Perhaps my narra-tive could be used as evidence if he's ever caught . . .

H.H.   (undated postcard)

What an astounding sequel. Quite fascinating, but rather alarming to think that there are such clever cons . . .

J.S.S.   2/4/68

. . . There's a further joke to add to *Trade*. I spent half an hour or so with Rosemary in New Scotland Yard early this

morning, and was asked to leaf through four albums of criminal photographs. There must have been fifteen hundred, a
real Thieves' Gallery. These albums drew a blank, and it was
only in Album 4 that one photograph hinted at a resemblance
to X. The policeman seemed interested and needed to make
sure how close the resemblance might be ("If you're sure, we
can arrest whoever it is") Not terribly close, I said. Well, he
replied, let's look at who you've got; he picked out the photograph and smiled. That's Bruce Reynolds, only train robber
on the loose. Last we heard of him, he was in South America.
Big reward for you if we catch him.

No, X was not Bruce Reynolds, but he's still free and using
the HH cheque book round the West End.

H.H. 4/4/68

. . . Anne and I were v. sorry you couldn't come on Sunday
[from the Essex–Suffolk border, where I'd been staying the
weekend] though you would have found us buried in poly-
thene bags full of rubbish. I would like to have shown you
some books that have got to be sold – though I suppose you
would not have been allowed to buy them from such a tainted
source . . .

I was bowled over by the latest instalment of the great
shop robbery. Surely Handy *must* have awarded you the
S. Holmes medal?

PS I had a mysterious letter, posted in SW1, which only
had in it an obituary of Anne's mother. There were some mistakes in it about "who she was" which had been underlined
in red ink. My name and address on the envelope had been
printed in ink – to disguise handwriting. What does your
sleuthwork say to that? Witchcraft? If so, why?

H.H.   19/4/68

I see there is a p.c. from you to Eddie. He has been away for over a week (fleeing before the invasion of Easter children). He comes back tomorrow and then is off to Greece after ten days. I have a feeling he won't now want *The Shipwreck* [which he'd ordered several months earlier] as he's going to have to take a great cargo back with him. He is a bad answerer anyway . . .

J.S.S.   21/4/68

Many thanks for letting me know about Eddie's *Shipwreck* – it was a slim chance at best . . .

Two proofs have come my way that I must try to put aside for you when everyone else has dipped in: John Lehmann on the three Sitwells,[90] *A Nest of Tigers*, very professional, using secondary, published sources but no new material [unlike the later *Façades* by John Pearson] . . . I've written a note of appreciation to J. Lehmann pointing out a frightful howler which had crept into the proof. In listing Edith S.'s friends, he names "Henry Cecil (Judge Leon) and his wife, Jeanne Stonor, a fellow-Catholic", which would raise a few eyebrows in Gray's Inn Square and Stonor.

The other proof (not out till the autumn) is Montgomery Hyde's *Henry James at Home*.

Christopher Sykes[91] has taken a huge swipe at the Brian Howard book in the May *Encounter*, and Handy is rubbing his hands. We've sold about 75 copies and it's almost out of print, but I'm sorry for M-J [Lancaster] that she should now come in for such swashbuckling.

---

90. Sir Osbert, Dame Edith and Sir Sacheverell Sitwell.
91. Christopher Sykes (1907–86), biographer.

Paul Getty Jr has opened an account, and Mr X has run up £600 worth of debts in the West End using our cheque book.

J.S.S.   24/4/68

X was caught by the CID yesterday and we had a visit from two officers this afternoon, who collected a list of the cheques so far forged. He comes up for trial next Wednesday.

Two extra facts to end the story:

i) That he performed exactly the same con at John Sandoe[92] on a Saturday morning. X picked up *Brian Howard* upstairs, then went into an hour and a half rigmarole with JS himself downstairs and, when he'd put together a heavy order, asked if he could be given cash for his "duplicate" copy of *BH*, again, "bought by his wife". Sandoe gave him the money and has been feeling sour and sore ever since. I wouldn't have heard about this if the J[onathan] Cape traveller who sometimes works at Sandoe hadn't arrived at the shop at just the same time as the CID officers.

ii) That X has been in a mental home and escaped fairly recently. It's very difficult to keep him there because he can trick the confidence of the warders. Look what happens when he's given innocent booksellers.

Now for a classic Mollie-ism. She was fairly bitchy about the policemen and the X *affaire*, but that was nothing to her rubbish this morning. It started with the letter to J. Lehmann pointing out what I saw as a mistake, but may have been no more than an ambiguity. Goodness knows why I leapt to the wrong conclusion, but my letter had been complimentary, and J.L. could not possibly have been offended. He came in yesterday and I apologized properly . . . I was hardly prepared

---

92. John Sandoe, the distinguished Chelsea bookshop, founded in 1957.

for Mollie's unanswerable speech as she swept off to the bank this morning:

'I hope you're properly ashamed of yourself . . . making the shop a laughing-stock round the dinner-tables of London. To write to John Lehmann without even asking Handy: people have been sacked for less than that. And to associate yourself with the shop in this – I think it's hard enough that you associate yourself with the shop at all."

If that happens once a week for ten years, I will be in a mental home by the time I'm 40, and I will plan cons against anyone who keeps accurate accounts.

H.H. 21/5/68

. . . I found Paris so expensive that I spent most of [my time] in the metro. One day, while in it, I found I was blinking and smarting and thought, oh it must be dustier than usual. Then I noticed other blinkers and later Nancy read out from the Figaro that quite a lot of the students' gas had penetrated underground. I've since felt quite proud of my whiff. A letter in that cramped handwriting arrived while I was at Nancy's – a shop bill with alas not enough stamps on – a thing which Nancy has a particular quirk about (one arrived the next morning for me from Anne – similarly understamped. Luckily I noticed the chalk and handed over 70 centimes). I implored N. not to remark because KNEW that it would be Rosemary who would be shot at dawn – but am afraid my words had no effect. Even though she rather delighted me by referring to the Bs as the MACBETHS . . .

J.S.S. 31/5/68

I'm off to Venice and Dalmatia later this evening . . . My apologies for not writing for ages. I've been non-stop for the last few weeks and I'm looking forward to a rest. Liz was away for a fortnight in Florence – very social as half the usual Garden crowd seems to have been there cherishing her words of operatic wisdom – and Handy gave me the shop to run. All too often I remembered your judging him a fraud, but only once did I let off any steam and I suppose he took some notice thereafter. His immediate reaction couldn't have been stuffier: "I come here very early in the morning and you will just have to get used to my being able to take walks. I am an old gentleman & mmm, mmm."

A couple of young Astors[93] approached me two weeks ago about starting a bookshop in the Fulham Road. You know the likely set-up: they had money to invest, I gather about £12000, and without actually wanting to see it go down a financial drain, they hoped to get some fun out of a world that would suit them, and what better than books? A social friend of theirs was putting up a third of the money and wanted to learn about bookselling from a professional, and they asked me if such a professional might consider coming to work under these terms: fairly full independence, a decent salary, and a shop of his own to start from scratch. They had some illusions which had to be shattered and I'm not sure that my cold water hasn't dowsed the scheme for good. They would have lost money immediately – bad premises and money spent on the wrong priorities – and I didn't like the sound of the social friend: not another Henry, but a dabbler.

Henry has announced that he will come and work in the shop 18 months before Handy retires. He has been a figure of enigma for almost three months, and Buck speculation has reached new depths of meanness . . .

Mollie has been expelled from her garden committee [Barkston Gardens]. How could the Barkstonians know the truth? It's taken such a short time to emerge.

---

93. David Astor (b. 1943), and James (b. 1945).

An excerpt from HH life this morning. I ask Liz if she wants the proof of Bob G[athorne] H[ardy]'s book on Amalfi. "No" comes straight back, though there was a time v. recently when she longed for it. Handy reaches for *A Farewell to Arms* and sits himself on a pile of books by the stairs.

H. And who came from Amalfi?

Blankness and apathy.

H. Rinaldi. You really ought to remember.

Liz: Oh, I could never read Hemingway again . . .

H. You can't say that, you really must have come off the boil.

Liz: Quite unreadable, his style's appalling.

H. (on a high horse) But his style's so hot, it's just a real winning number . . . And, what is more, he invented it which is more than you can say of most.

Liz: And a great deal of harm it's done.

. . . No time to tell you about the Bucks' social climacteric, the eightieth birthday party for Guy and Lettie [Benson]. "The Duchess of Rutland[94] was looking so WONDERFUL . . . I loved some of those clothes."

H.H. 15/6/68

. . . You must give me more details of the grand social climacteric. I'm sure that the Duchess of Rutland was a poppet, as well as quite my most favourite person.

I do hope Yugoslavia was a success and has fortified you to face those jolly shopmates. Last time I went to London I was Trumpered by Mr Johnson[95] (him being a Cypriot I thought he might give ME some tips – for a change). As I was quite certain would happen, Handy was the person immediately before me and had stayed on to let off gas over some

---

94. The Duchess of Rutland, née Frances Sweeny.
95. Mr Johnson was head barber at Trumper's of 9 Curzon Street.

General in a neighbouring cell. I could hear the gas hissing and, when at last it stopped, he had to pass where I was being shorn. Of course Mr J said to him "Look who is here." It was a fearful shock for all and I have never seen H before turn a deep crimson. He had his surface amiability but there was no invitation to come in after – it was anyhow too near gin time – so I kept clear.

I start on my crazy travels on 28 June. Ten days with Osbert [Sitwell] (unless put off. Silence for some time). Then join Anne's train in Venice for Athens. One night there, then boat on to Cyprus – may be away till mid-September.

J.S.S.   18/6/68

Back from Yugoslavia in the middle of last night, and much cheered by your letter before facing the full orchestra today. In a fortnight one almost forgets that the Ghastlies are so permanent; I'd had such a marvellous rest and change that I returned in hearty enough spirits for the enemy to enjoy putting on the dampers . . . Mollie will complain before the end of the week that I never stop talking about my boring holiday to everyone . . . What, said Handy, was that pile of extremely scruffy postcards that arrived unsolicited a week or so ago? Did I mean to encourage that side of the business he was trying to run it down and he would be obliged if I planned to do something different? The postcards (sepia Edwardian views) . . . included one of Split, two of Dubrovnik and five of Sarajevo, seventy or eighty in all and they cost the shop £1.

[This weekend] I was provisionally asked to stay in Dedham with a delightful family called Erith;[96] as I took their youngest daughter Laura to Yugoslavia, I've every reason to

---

96. Raymond Erith (1904–73), the leading Classical architect of his generation, and his wife Pamela (1910–87).

believe in their delightfulness. I'm rather disappointed that I shall have to go home to Oxford instead as my parents disappear on holiday next week . . .

H.H.   undated [from Montegufoni]

Harold Acton and his German boy friend have just been to lunch. Harold gave some account of Liz's triumphal Florentine progress, writing the life of Mario[97] and visiting Mario's house. He said how she had been "taken up" by a couple called Cummings (American queers I rather hazily gathered though may be wrong). Harold described Liz as "touching" which is the last adjective I would choose (and rather doubt if you would) but, if one starts telling truth, what's the point? Nobody believes it and they just write one off as a blighted bitch. It's less wounding to do some muffled clapping and then write all about it to you – because there is nobody else on earth to whom the truth is known except Anne. Also current about Liz is the popular heart of gold myth. Harold said about Mollie "What a REFINED woman she is" in his rather mouthing voice. "I believe her maiden name was Freeze-Green" he went on. "No, it was CATLOO," I answered and said no more.

As a matter of fact Osbert does have quite a perception about shop truths and, when alone with him, I have let hair down quite some way. He doesn't seem all that much worse than when I saw him last, I suppose about two years ago, though it is a sad figure huddled in his wheel-chair. My chief difficulty – as I thought it would be – is hearing him – though he is patient when one doesn't. Thank God there is a permanent male nurse – especially as, today, Frank[98] (the Malt.

97. *Mario and Grisi* was published in 1985.
98. Frank Magro.

valet risen to sec[retary]), cocky and bossy but genuinely fond of O[sbert], has gone off for his holiday. He's indispensable so I feel responsible without him though we get through the evening quite happily – sitting on the terrace and me reading *What Maisie Knew* out loud (O. has to be wheeled off to pee by the nurse quite often). It is delightful to be almost a prisoner in the castle – no means of getting anywhere (there's no castle car) and nothing one HAS to do – except to sit with O. and wander among the boiling vineyards. It is a little bit eerie at night. I am in a bedroom which is all by itself in a wing – up two narrow stone staircases and through a series of anterooms.

Frank told me that rumour reached Osbert that Handy had told John Lehmann that his *Nest of Tigers* is doing marvellously well, but had told Sachie that it has ruined O's reputation. O. is very upset about it . . .

H.H. [2/7/68]

I did a little secretary work for O. this morning and typed a few letters which he dictated. He does hear from the maddest people. There was one this morning from a woman in Birmingham saying she thought she would have got on v. well with Edith and then adding "I myself do not care for artists of any description . . ." and further on, "I do not like to be plucked at in the street."

Send me one of your shop bulletins if you have a moment. I do enjoy them. Now I suppose the Bs are away. What lucky country have they patronized this year? . . .

H.H. 8/8/68 [from Kyrenia, picture postcard of icon painters in Cyprus]

I rather think they would run up a fore-edge, so would take the order (for a commission of course). . . All is splendid except I may be summoned home because of a dying aunt. We had a drink in Lapithos with a customer of yours (Dr [Paul] Wilkinson[99]).

By the time I wrote again to Heywood, almost two months had passed; he was a long way away and, as I explained rather pompously, "A girl whom one wants to marry takes up much time." I tried to make up with accumulated anecdotes.

J.S.S.   12/8/68

. . . Mollieism [for you], even if you are 1000 miles away and Buchananry for the moment irrelevant. She hadn't made a speech to me for some months and I should have been warned, and not mildly cheered, by her abstinence. The incident that sparked it was typical. Lady Gowrie[100] had been talking merrily to me in the front of the shop and had picked up [Pamela Hansford Johnson's] *Survival of the Fittest*. Turning slightly away from me, she asked in Handy's direction "what the maestro thought about this one". Picking up her jolly mood, I said "Oh well the maestro, you know, never reads a novel." She laughed and was a little surprised to see Handy's hackles visibly rise: you may remember how he somehow hunches up like a little armadillo and his voice takes on that bully-me-if-you-like-but-it-won't-get-you-any-where-'cos-I'm-the-boss-round-these-parts tone. He said, "Well, I don't know about that. I've of course had a *good look* at it, and I came to the conclusion that it didn't really come off." Lady G bought something else and left, in high good humour.

---

99. Dr Wilkinson was graphically described by Frances Partridge in *Good Company*.
100. Xandra Bingley (b. 1942), literary agent.

No word followed from H. I nipped downstairs and told Mr Stafford that I'd got a rare shaft into the boss's armour and I expected to pay for it sooner or later. For the time being, I rather enjoyed Handy having taken offence at something so incredibly trivial.

Penalty came in the middle of last week. Mollie waited till no one was in the shop and then said:

'Some things worry me about you in the shop. Why was it you said the other day to Lady Gowrie that Handy never read a book? He was *of course* upset about it, and so was I, and you often seem to give the impression that you're working against other people in the shop. Handy gets this impression as well and I get very worried about it. Things do tick up against you, you know . . . and we really cannot have this disloyalty to everyone else."

I copied this down, my fingers shaking, as soon as I was out of sight.

Liz has not been behaving too overpoweringly, and we managed to stay on very reasonable terms when the Bs were in France. They went for a change to their special hotel in Beynac [where] they made an *extraordinarily* interesting contact, some Frog major who'd been on Maurois' staff in 1945. It sounded as if H. had received a thorough contribution to his knowledge, deeply-based and multifaceted though it is already, of Second World War history.

Meanwhile, back at the ranch, doubtless guided by their telepathic inspiration, we managed to sell an amazing number of second-hand and antiquarian books – at a time when H. could not conceivably take the credit, and when there were very few decent new books coming through from the publishers. Muriel Spark has rounded off her collection of Max-iana, a man called [Alistair] McAlpine[101] has started a serious col-

---

101. Lord McAlpine of West Green (b. 1942), collector and writer.

lection of Victoriana, no standard [literary] set stays in the shop longer than a week, anything Pre-Raph. disappears in a trice, and the shelves are emptier than I ever remember them. In fact I went on an expedition to the Guildhall Bookshop in Surbiton *during shop hours* to try to find some reasonable children's stock – which I've managed to do, despite having chosen the wettest morning of a very wet August. Having taken great trouble to get back before rumours were mongered, I was particularly pleased by Mollie's only comment, when I had had time simply to open my post, deal with some customers for Victoriana, go out for and return from lunch: "And why is it that he leaves his wedding invitations all among his Clique reports?"

Am I to visit other shops only on the odd Saturday afternoon, as I've done in Colchester and Stratford in the last few weeks? . . .

PS I wonder what P. B. Wilkinson is like in his natural habitat. He might be rather a bore, as he holds a high opinion of his own eccentricity.

H.H.   28/9/68

There are various excuses why I have not responded to your enjoyable last bulletin, the chief one being that you only put a ninepenny stamp on it so that it took three weeks to arrive by surface mail and only arrived just before we left Cyprus. Surely *EVERYBODY* knows that Cyprus is considered to be the Middle East so that a shilling (it may have risen) stamp is *essential* for airmail. Actually, nobody did know and I rather wonder whether Everybody herself knows.

We have now been back here for a fortnight. I keep saying to myself that it is nice to be home again though I am not yet convinced. It seems dank and sombre after sunny Cyprus and then we are having a time getting the house straight after some abominable tenants. They had a gang of boy children who set up a stall by the drive gate full of our objects from the house. They did a roaring trade with passing motorists.

Then I had to go up to London with Sheila to clear out the flat of my aunt Knox who had died. That was a very unrewarding job. There were hundreds of newpaper parcels in cupboards which, when one got inside, contained things like feathers for pillows and flannelette protectors for my late Uncle Robert's stump.

I did get to Trumper's early one morning, chiefly in order to tell Mr Johnson news of Cyprus. Afterwards I stared through the shop window, feeling rather like the Victorian urchin gazing at a Christmas tree. First I saw you and nearly decided to come in but then I saw the Beadle popping up from downstairs – so I scampered. Actually, I decided it was too early in the morning for any choir to have to start singing.

You were wondering whether we found Dr Wilkinson a bore. Well, the first time (or the 2nd) we went there, we decided he was a crasher. We were aching for a drink but he had arranged in his drawing-room an exhibition of books on St Helena (Frances Partridge [who was staying] has just translated a book about the place) which we were made to go very slowly round immediately on arrival. However, we saw quite a lot of him and were gradually won over. He's a genuine eccentric as well as being kind-hearted and, sometimes, very funny. Amazingly erudite. If skilfully steered on to subjects that interest oneself, he is rewarding – though I don't say that large doses wouldn't be too much. Anne and I asked him to lunch one day and bought a chicken. On what we thought was the day before, we had just finished our lunch when he turned up. (It was so timeless there that we had become out of date.) What was worse was that our telegram inviting him had got the time wrong – 1.45 instead of 12.45, so when he arrived he was absolutely famished. All we could do was to rush him up an omelette. It was a proof of his good nature that he took it all extremely well and appeared very amused.

I was plunged into a quandary almost immediately after getting back here by being rung up by Derek Verschoyle[102] to ask if I would manage his Woodbridge bookshop (he has bought the Ancient House Bookshop in Ipswich, so cannot run them both). I felt that I OUGHT to accept as the cash would be welcome, especially after the extravagant holiday. However, after a day or two of thinking, I decided – rather guiltily – that D.V. isn't sympathetic enough to work with. He must be mad, don't you think, at his age, to be buying bookshops right and left.

It is good news that you are still making assaults on East Anglia and I send best wishes for their success. Can you come down for a weekend . . . perhaps you would like to bring her over to lunch?

J.S.S.   7/10/68

A note in haste to say that I've had a week's holiday and returned to London yesterday, that I much enjoyed your letter and that I will be getting engaged to Laura Erith, officially on Thursday. We had a splendid time church-crawling in Kilvert country, then dashed most of the way across England to ask permission of her father in Dedham . . .

There was at least a week's work to be fitted in to today and I'm feeling fairly pulverized. Handy and Liz had really had a go of it last week, as Rosemary has left us for good and a new secretary, Setitia Butler,[103] arrives tomorrow. They seemed quite pleased to have me back, and may take a day or two to return to their normal. I saved my news until mid-

---

102. Derek Verschoyle (1911–73), publisher.
103. Setitia Butler (b. 1946), bookseller, with her husband Anthony Simmonds.

afternoon [which] produced some brilliant banalities from Handy. Paternal advice from one who knows all: "Do you share the same interests, one?" and "Have you got the same sense of 'umour, two? If you haven't got those, then you might as well jump down the drain; but if you have, then you can probably do those things that you will be able to do when you are married . . . I've been married twice and nearly married on a number of occasions, so I speak if not *ex-cathedra*, at least from somewhere like that."

H.H.   10/10/68

What very splendid news. Many true congratulations and wishes from Anne and me. I felt it was in the air but did not realize how near to a happy landing. I think now my assault language was a little crude . . . Of course I much enjoyed the Sage's cathedral sermon.

PS I have got a few children's books for sale – but we won't refer to such a subject unless you are inclined for smuggling.

J.S.S.   11/10/68

Very many thanks for your sweet letter. Everybody's been very kind, with one notable exception. Mollie must have heard the news on Monday. I hoped she might approach me when she first arrived on Wed. Not a word, only grumbles about accounts, dollars and wages – until it came for her to give me my envelope of money (always her favourite moment for a broadside). Then "John, I hear you're engaged again . . .?"[104] "Yes," gasping. "Is it any different from last time?" "Of course it is, entirely different, etc." Further ques-

---

104. I had been engaged in 1965 to Ann Cooke-Yarborough, who broke it off during my first few weeks at Heywood Hill.

tions on whether she's *rich* ("I hope she is") and what she does ("Handy says she weaves") and what her name is ("Oh, Laura's quite a nice name.")

No need to garble this, as I know you can imagine it: not a single hint of congratulation. I shall have to thicken my armour for the future . . .

No further exchange in 1968, except for a postcard from H.H. on 28 December about a date when Laura and I might come over to lunch. "My desk is deep in drift so that I cannot remember which day you suggested . . . hoping to see you and all stigamata (I shall leave that extra A – it somehow helps) . . ."

1969

Up to this point I have kept details of my non-bookshop life out of the story. Heywood was not likely to be interested and, at this distance, there is little that is worth recording. I had lived in Chiltern Street since the spring of 1966. This flat had been a lucky find: it was directly north of 10 Curzon Street and could be reached on a brisk walk morning and evening via Grosvenor and Manchester Squares. I had shared the flat initially with a first cousin, Anthony Bottrall, but he was posted abroad in 1967 and thereafter I'd had lodgers, the longest-lasting of whom were Alan and Gillie Howarth, the friends who'd married in Dublin in October 1967. After their wedding they invited themselves for three weeks while they looked for married quarters, and stayed for an enjoyable thirteen months.

Now engaged, Laura and I needed to redecorate the flat before our wedding in late March. Laura was living in Airlie Gardens W8, and through a cold winter we each spent a good deal of time on the 27 bus. My letters to Heywood became less frequent not least because I now had a sympathetic ear close at hand.

Laura, her parents and I had all driven over to Snape during the New Year break.

H.H.   5/1/69

. . . It was nice seeing you. Both Anne and I felt that you are much more secure in the shop – which pleased us both very much. We liked Laura and we liked her parents – and, altogether, we were delighted by all that is happening to you (I can hear Harriet or Lucy [their daughters] saying "Don't be so impossibly patronizing").

H.H.   22/1/69

I found myself near Peter Jones [where we had a wedding list] last Friday, and not knowing when I could be found there again, as well as great danger of meeting Mollie in CARPETS, I thought I would get over the Bride's Book – but not so easy. I am still not out of the wood. I sat at the table – a lone ranger among Brides and Brides' mothers – to study Laura's list and thought how, as being on the groom's side, I must discover an item mildly masculine. Sherry glasses or goblets or balloons (brandy). Downstairs you go with your slip they said to the proper department. So down I went to GLASS, avoiding CARPETS, and a lady said she would HELP. But she found that she could not. She went to a drawer where the proper sort of glass, goblet or balloon should be but it was empty. It was then that I turned into a nasty customer and said that, when a bride has an item on her list, it surely should be kept in stock. However, I recovered myself and, remembering my former life, said no doubt they would be having them in again VERY SOON. She said no doubt and in meantime she would write to Miss Erith to say I had ordered them. I said don't do that, it would be premature, and besides I want them sent to the groom. This morning I get a letter from P. Jones to say that the sherry glasses (I decided on them, sadly thinking from own experience how seldom balloons and goblets become filled) are still out of stock but that they have "written to the Bride advising her of your gift". That made me think how I should never get straight unless I wrote you a full confession . . .

You said that you had meant to ask advice as to whether you should ask the V[yner]s to the w[edding]. I have been thinking hard about that and my advice on the whole would be yes. I think that it's fairly safe that they wouldn't come, that it's just possible they would send a present, that it's politic to keep yourself well IN VIEW with them – all these horrid reasons. It might be a bit awkward if they wrote to us and said could they stay here for it but – even if they did – Anne and I would stick to our sad Cinderella decision [to refuse the invitation].

J.S.S.   27/1/69

. . . The first hint [of your adventures at P. Jones] was a week ago when Laura rang me and said in a voice of great puzzlement that we had been signed in for some [sherry] glasses by S. H. Hill, and who on earth could that be? Well, not for nothing do I sign your name fifteen times a day (even if I didn't spend the war in a decoding department[105]) and I imagined that a salesman might well not have appreciated the subtleties of your palsied G . . .

I had learned of Earl Evans's[106] visit [to Snape] the day after he saw you: we fortunately bumped into each other in Lancaster Passage. I suggested that H[andy] would not exactly leap with joy if he was told news of life at the Priory, and I gather that E.E. kept mum. So mum in fact that the only evidence of his visit was that he'd been cudgelled into taking H.B.'s favourite book, *The Black Death*, and a scrofulous piece of paper had appeared on my desk saying that he wanted *A Story of a Failure* by Brian Howell.

Liz was away last week and I just kept head above water: the rain almost wrecked the roof [at the back of the shop] during Wed. afternoon . . . Still no squeak from Henry, tho' he's seeing Handy tomorrow. Handy's preparing to take *a very tough* line, weakened though he is by diverticulitis (and

---

105. This refers to Handy's wartime job in Press Censorship.
106. Dr Earl Evans (1910–99), biochemist from the University of Chicago, and very loyal shop customer.

gin). The work he does at the moment is laughable: Mollie even asked me on Friday whether I thought we could fit someone else on the staff. She managed to get in a few shafts at me when she opened the shop *in loco mariti*, but she's a bit worried.

H.H.   8/2/69

I know that this is a very bad time to be asking you the following questions – you will be full of wedding affairs in any spare moments – also I hear from Betty B[atten] that you've been having 'flu . . . The thing is that my cousin Elizabeth Johnstone has asked me if I will value her library at Trewithen. She only wants a valuation of the books as a whole – not one by one – so I think that a rough idea would satisfy her. – She would of course pay a fee – though, being a cousin, I don't think I can ask more than £10 . . . If I do undertake it, I will have to spend a day or two in London looking at B[ook] A[uction] R[ecords] in the B. Museum. If I do that, perhaps . . . might I ask your advice about any fearful problems that might arise? I know that a lot of her books are valuable. There are some colour-plate ones – including those exotic butterflies. More problematic would be the early books on Cornwall and 17th cent. ones about houses . . .

PS I see I have been spelling your name wrong for years. More forgiveness.

H.H.   15/2/69

Many thanks for letter [since lost] and for saying that you might help a bit over auntie's library . . .

How awful for you having to do all that scraping [of walls] by night. I find all do-it-yourself activities intolerable and, when I try, things become more UNdone than ever.

Of course, the day before your letter came [telling Heywood that the Buchanans had chosen to refuse our wedding invitation] Anne had written to Mrs Erith refusing. If you really think that it would be all right and that there won't be some bugging person, we would love to come. Might it be wise to leave it open in case some impediment arises – I nearly said in case of buggery (doesn't to bug mean to spy in modern language?) – I begin to doubt myself.

I am so glad to hear that the Bs have "brassed up" . . . [A characteristic Handy-ism. They had given us a present of £20 which we promptly spent on Pevsner's *Buildings of England*.]

H.H.   21/2/69

Elizabeth Johnstone has sent me the catalogue of the Trewithen library. I was appalled when it arrived, as it's in 4 vols – though not quite so bad when I looked into it – about 50 pages a vol. and only about 6 books on each page. Don't begin to quake with the thought that I may be going to send it to you . . .

H.H.   15/3/69

Your letter [lost] arrived by the same post as the errant list [of books] from Angela C[ulme] S[eymour].[107] I knew it had erred because I saw her the next day at the wedding and she said she would post it on. How it managed to escape at her flat, I can't think . . . I can't possibly expect you to do anything about the list in this week of all weeks. I do have a copy in case it does any more escaping. See you on THE DAY.

---

107. One of Anne Hill's oldest friends.

H.H.   [8/4/69, picture postcard from Skye)

Many thanks for the list which I had not imagined you'd be able to do so quickly. A great help.

It has been wonderful here – picnics among lochs and islands in blazing sun. The bolted wife of our absent host was an old shop customer whom I remember getting the full hissing treatment from M[ollie] because of a terrible mutual affair.

P.S. Had just finished the p.c. when I thought it seemed bleak not to say how much Anne and I enjoyed the wedding. We did. We were introduced by Jenny [Lipscomb]'s father to John Raven and he gave us some useful "tips" about here – where best to walk etc.

Mr S[tafford] was touching about champagne. He told us he had never had any and that he didn't think he'd like it and was there any beer? A little bit later he said it was the best drink he'd ever drunk.

J.S.S.   21/4/69

I hope that Buster [Brown]'s[108] safely arrived by now; Mr Stafford had entered you on the postal sheet as Mr Mundham of Suffolk. Alan [Allan][109] of Kettlebaston says that you wrote to him two or three years ago about B. Brown, so his telepathy is not as phenomenal as you imagined. I've had a real lucky break as a result of my visit to him. When I saw him 10 days ago, I found, on top of a pile near his desk, a folio part of what purported to be a Walter Crane bible. I'd never

---

108. A series of American illustrated books for children featuring a bulldog, Buster Brown.
109. Second-hand bookseller working from his home, Kettlebaston Hall, near Hadleigh, Suffolk.

heard of such a thing being printed . . . so the 12th Part, which had most of Proverbs and the last bit of Psalms (with illustrations taken from all over the Bible, even one from the N.T.), must have been some sort of sample. Allan hinted that he might know of more material from a Crane bible . . . and today he brought a vast bound folio, cover design, endpapers, title-page, all the letter-pieces and even 1 or 2 full-page illustrations by Crane; called The Holy Bible, but quite incomplete, at least minus Psalms and Proverbs, and no N.T. at all, with five copies of the publisher's prospectus tucked into the front endpapers. So I must do a lot of research . . .

H.H. 13/5/69

I am absolutely delighted to be crowned with success[110] (so unlike last night's nightmare, which I will tell you about). The crown being a little shaky only makes it the more suitable for Anne's elderly cousin, Helen Haviland, to whom I shall now be able to send it as a reward for having us to stay. She has been asking for that book for years. It seems a bit unfair on Setitia that she should supply me with free rewards, but will you tell her that she has done a really kind deed which will bring much pleasure and that I am very grateful.

I went down to Cornwall the weekend before last and valued my cousin's library. I turned down a fee in the end (except I let her pay the railway fare), as I found that I had valued it at exactly the sum she had insured it for – seventeen thousand pounds. Could you just bear to look up one more book for me? . . . I shall type it on a plain piece of paper so that you can take it to Curzon St. without my contaminating address . . .

---

110. The shop had traced a second-hand copy of *Crowned with Success*.

During last night I found myself back in the shop which seemed to be so seething with assistants that there was no room for me to sit even at my old underground desk [in the Print Room]. One of my most tiresome friends came in who said he had smashed the disgusting ivory miniature of Shelley which Sangorski[111] had painted and appallingly ruined his first edition by sinking it in the binding. He had brought back the bits and said I was to return the whole thing to Hobson. There was a dread hush from the assisters (you were NOT among them), and I knew that the Pope was about to excommunicate me . . .

J.S.S.   16/5/69

How is this for silly fibbery? I heard Mollie talking to Handy about the Holman Hunt exhib. at the V & A – Private View Wed. evening – and saying that surely they couldn't face going: too many people, and really it would be so much quieter if she could go alone on Thursday morning. So in a conversational way I said that Laura and I had thought we would be going that evening. I thought no more of it, until Setitia said a little later: "I hear that Mollie and Handy won't go to the V & A Private View *because you're going*."

There's also been trouble about a proof of *Akenfield*.[112] I'd been given it, had read and enjoyed it, and had passed it on to Raymond Erith. Mollie and Handy went to a party to launch the book, found it infested with The Young, and M. gave Mr Marshall [the publisher's rep.] a monumental blast for not sending a proof. She asked me next day if I had read it and whether I had the proof. Yes, I said. No one had ever told me that you wanted it. "Surely you know I'm interested in any-

111. Sangorski and Sutcliffe, bookbinders, of Poland Street W1. Mr Hobson was its manager.
112. Ronald Blythe's book about a composite village in Suffolk.

thing to do with East Anglia, and diverted by village life . . ." "Oh well," said I, "I'm sorry you haven't had it, I'll get it to you as soon as I can . . . and if you're interested, there's a marvellous autobiography coming out about that part of the world in three or four weeks time." "Oh yes, what is it called?" "*Reuben's Corner*,"[113] and warming to my subject, "it's by someone whose father was a farm labourer at the time of the First War . . ." At this moment Handy appeared at the top of the stairs. Mollie turned to him, cutting me off with "Isn't it nice the way John tells *me* about the book-trade?" . . .

We had a *very* good evening with Henry and Margaret [Vyner] last week; they were on the friendliest form and exceedingly nice to Laura . . .

H.H.   19/5/69

. . . The latest pettifoggeries of the Pope's wife made Anne and me gasp – though we couldn't help being fascinated.

R. Vanderbilt suddenly appeared here on Saturday (I couldn't remember if he should be called Robert or Bob, and I believe I chose the wrong one, Robert). I expect he will innocently tell the Bs and there will be fearful hissings that he should have been on Tom Tiddler's ground. I gathered from him that he is financing them in Switzerland;[114] hissings will have to be confined to the Vatican.

H.H.   26/5/69

. . . We are just off to a gala at Framlingham – for the benefit of Algy [a grandson] because there will be the RAF

---

113. Spike Mays' memoir of his childhood in west Suffolk.
114. The Vanderbilts then lived in Switzerland and could "lend" money to the Buchanans for their holiday to get round the currency restrictions on foreign travel.

Band and balloon races. Archaeologists are digging in the garden but so far they have only unearthed Uncle Eddie's gin bottles.

You will of course have gathered that those filthy books did in the end find their way to Handy. So I suppose that those desk drawers are more stuffed and bursting than ever – or do they still moulder away in the vellum suitcase in which they arrived? I sent the address of the owner to Henry and asked him either to pass it on to Handy or to send him a cheque himself (£40 I believe). I'll be amazed if anything has really happened and of course the poor man's suitcase is certain to be "a dead loss". In my usual role of unrewarded buffer, I can see that I am going to be thoroughly buffed at both ends. . . .

J.S.S.   16/6/69

In the later part of Saturday morning, Handy gave me a long-awaited glimpse of the shop's future, now that Henry has failed to sell out to W. H. Smith . . . There is no immediate guarantee that I will manage the shop, nor will he encourage anyone being taken onto the staff as an understudy: he won't have alien figures being introduced while *he's* around. And he reckons that without the great triumvirate – tho' he only mentions the great I AM – the shop could not possibly be viable: he does x percentage of the turn-over, and I do y, and the result of his going would mean a loss of z, but he wasn't going to say any more for the moment . . . He then moved on to the second half of his monologue, all worked out to the finest detail, and in no way admitting of response, let alone adjustment. . . . "You may be good at this and that, but you do not appear to realize how much work I did at the time I was your age. I was running a shop from top to bottom etc. etc. And it seems to me that there are two boats at Heywood Hill, in one of which you'd find me and Mollie and Liz, the other rowed by JSS." "Is this surprising?" I said, "If this was so, it could be explained by one boat having existed for twenty years, the other having only recently been accepted." This changed the subject. "The trouble is," he went on, "and you probably don't realize this yourself, that you correct us all as if you were a headmaster (oh! oh!), that your tone of voice becomes almost canonical . . ." As an illustration of my non-cooperation in shop affairs, there were these flower-prints – and he went over to the folder of Trew's *Plantae Selectae* – , which I'd badgered him to price when he'd bought them, and who did he find were his first customers, Laura and me? Didn't I understand that he wanted to make money out of them and what use were we as customers? . . . He has tried to be awfully nice to me today. I suppose I prefer him in this mood, but it's a pretty fearful alternative . . .

Heywood had been passing on parts of my letters for several months to Nancy Mitford, swearing her to silence. In his next letter (of 1 July) he quoted N.M.'s feelings about the Shop Row, that she never understood it and never wanted to "because I so madly wished to hunt with the hare and run with the hounds". He went on: "I suppose that Mollie, like [a character in] some early Verdi opera, will keep up her remorseless vendetta and smear campaign until her dying day. I realize that Henry has been a doubtful asset but, as the Bs were always pining to be rid of me and as they got such immensely favourable contracts, I cannot see (though can well imagine) what vile horror story about me Mollie spreads. Any normal civilized person would have buried any hatchets long ago and we could all have helped one another in every direction . . ." He told me that he and Anne were going to the Vyners for the following weekend. A week later he reported that they had had a "very easy and jolly" time, and avoided shop talk. In this letter he quoted Anne's aunt,

Lady D. de V[esci] "asking me if I can explain the shop's behaviour to her old governess called Mouse". Handy had failed to put some drawings into Sotheby's on her behalf and, although the estimate had been £15, had sent her a cheque "for no more than £7-9-0. It seems an odd sort of business which loses the address of the owner of items for which they are responsible until they are sold and the transaction concluded . . ."

H.H. 17/8/69

I am sorry that I have been a long time returning this [Volume 4 of Edel's *Henry James*]. In the middle of reading it, I lent it to Benjamin Britten which I hope you won't mind, but he is writing an opera on H.J.'s short story *Owen Wingrave* and there is a bit about that. I enjoyed reading it very much but wasn't quite sure if it's as good as the earlier vols. A faint Americanism seems to creep in sometimes and some of his hypotheses and parallels seem far-fetched – like *Turn of the Screw* being mixed up with his move into Lamb House. I was particularly delighted to learn that H.J. was mad about the name SAXMUNDHAM.

Anne and I are off tomorrow to stay with [Lady] Mairi Bury[115] at Mount Stewart. Betty Batten will be there, also, I believe, Derek Hill and Robin McD[ouall] – so, what with the petrol bombs as well, it will be a real tinder box . . .

J.S.S. 20/8/69

. . . It's awful that I haven't written for so long. Liz was away for her fortnight after the Bs got back [from Switzerland] and I felt so flaked every evening that I couldn't put my

---

115. Lady Mairi Bury (b. 1921), daughter of the 7th Marquess of Londonderry.

mind to anything. The summer hasn't been comfortable for anyone in London. Least of all at no. 10 where Mollie got so sticky on her banking and dollar days that she had to have a fan installed in her back room. Which promptly went wrong, but it's now repaired and serves at least psychologically to circulate the Hot Air.

There have been times when I've almost felt myself In Favour with the Bs, by dint of some hard work clearing out the packing room and children's room. The latter now looks quite different: the central table has been replaced by a rectangular piece of furniture, made by Mr Stafford's father, with shelves on four sides. Of course new spaces create new problems, and everyone has his/her own idea of where to stock the books and how to display them. Mollie insisted that mine should be the master mind, while Setitia was away, but every move has been watched with extreme circumspection and all, except my actual throwing of unsaleable stuff, have been generally criticized. . . . Mollie says that I must [arrange returning books to publishers] now and take it out of Handy's (feeble enough) control. She has to make his excuses for him: "Of course if he was now running Harrods, he'd have an office and a carpet of his own and just wouldn't have to worry about things like the stock in the packing-room . . . you *are* the junior member of the staff and even if it is a thankless job, how can you possibly know about the shop without doing the jobs like this?"

Setitia sent Liz – a most diplomatic move – a cutting from an Irish paper showing Derek Hill laughing merrily with Annie Fleming[116] . . . It appeared to concern Jack B. Yeats, whose books we've been trying to trace for D.H. during the last few months . . .

116. Ann Fleming (1913–81), née Charteris, later Lady Rothermere.

The turnover for this year is just going to touch £100,000. A triumph for which Handy takes maximum credit, also a cut of the profits . . .

H.H.   25/9/69

. . . I am going to be a further bore and ask if, sometime during the next week or two, you could look up the following book in B[ook] A[uction] R[ecords]: Mrs Loudon. THE LADIES FLOWER GARDEN OF ORNAMENTAL BULBS. 1841. 4to, orig. cloth, gilt. I hadn't met [the owner] before (a hot keen yachtswoman though she's said to be "a dirty sailor" – whatever that means). College Gateway bookshop in Ipswich has offered her £50 for it which, in days of yore, would have been a good price but I suppose it may have gone whizzing up like everything else.

Your advice about the "dolls house" bore splendid fruit in the shape of a cheque for £15 and one of Handy's disarming letters saying that he was deeply sorry but mistakenly thought that I had already been paid for it. I was equally sly in my letter to him – describing it as an "Edwardian model of a house in a glass case" and saying that, if I did not hear from him that it had been sold, I would call to collect it . . . Answer by return.

J.S.S.   26/9/69

[My report on shop upsets was passed on to Nancy Mitford in Heywood's letter of 2 October. I also gave a brief account of our recent two-week holiday in Spain.]

. . . The Mrs Loudon was fetching £50 at auction two years ago, but the last B.A.R. suggests that it might be £70-£75 . . . [the owner] should probably stick out for £70, or else bring it to London.

According to Setitia, Handy smelt a rat about the doll's house, and it remains to be seen if he'll mention it. His excuse up till then was that it was *difficult* for him, as he was not on speaking terms with you . . . He is said to be on a new course of pills. They make him extra-energetic and extra-irritable. Not many manifestations of the first, plenty of the second.

H.H.   17/10/69

. . . It's news to me that I am supposed to be on non-speakers with Handy. Things seem to get madder and madder . . . I don't think that you should put Iris Origo's GIOVANNA & JANE[117] on the Clique. [While I had been on holiday, Heywood had asked Handy to advertise for this elusive children's book. Handy told him that it was Cliqued, but I found that it wasn't when I returned, and suspected a trap.] Something catastrophic might happen. It's rather a bore as Anne wants it badly because of Harriet going to live in Italy and the book being about an English child who goes there and makes friends with an Italian child. . . . Perhaps, some time after Gethsemane, I might send a card to the shop – addressed to nobody – and timidly suggest that it might be re-Cliqued. But I'll ask you what the temperature is first . . .

P.S. I bet there was an eruption when it was noticed that I had praised a book in an advert in the S. Times. It was sent to me by Raleigh Trevelyan[118] of Michael Joseph who said he thought I would enjoy it very much, which wasn't quite true, and then was appalled to see myself quoted in the advert. Perhaps it gave the Bs some satisfaction that I was bracketed with Godfrey Winn and Anna Neagle.[119]

---

117. *Giovanna and Jane*, published in 1947.
118. Raleigh Trevelyan (b. 1923), publisher and biographer.
119. Godfrey Winn (1908–71), journalist, and Dame Anna Neagle (1904–86), actress.

J.S.S.   24/10/69

... real drama at No. 10 a week ago ... I had felt a streaming cold about to start during Thursday afternoon, and warned Handy before I left that I might have to stay at home on Fri. I wasn't too well next morning, and it seemed better to try and throw it off away from the shop. Liz had been under fearful pressure for a couple of days, and despite doing many extra hours, had had precious little thanks from H. I hoped that they'd be able to cope without me. They weren't. At 1.30 p.m. the telephone rang: "John, it's Mollie, how bad is your cold?" No pause for an answer, then "Liz has broken down in hysterics, she's just left the shop, it was my fault, I know it was, but I don't care, it had to come ... I haven't told Handy that I was going to ring, so I'll put down the receiver as soon as he comes back; the shop's in turmoil, I don't know whether Liz is going to come back ..." Plonk down went the receiver. Well, my cold ... was definitely better so, sucker that I am, I rang Handy and asked if he'd like me to come in for a couple of hours and work downstairs. "Does this come from the blue?" he asked, so I told him it was Mollie's doing. And I went to the shop where Liz had pulled herself together – after sobbing in the loo for twenty minutes – , and I was given everyone's account of the trauma, and Mollie announced that she'd take a bet with anyone that Liz would be in an asylum by the time she was fifty ...

Someone wrote to us a few days ago about a translation of Gide's *Theseus* that you published, or did you only distribute?, in 1949. He was "doing a study of the Officina Bodoni"[120] and wanted information about this edition of *Theseus*, though I don't quite know how this is relevant. Best of all he'd have liked a copy ...

---

120. High-quality printers in Verona.

Have you managed to beg, borrow or steal the last Leonard Woolf?[121] It's so marvellous, and it got such a silly review from P[hilip] Toynbee.[122] I should have thought that the quintet wd. stand as a monument for ever, and that carping critics wd. look even sillier in a generation's time.

H.H.   13/11/69

. . . I enjoyed the engraved invitation from Sir George [Weidenfeld].[123] (It's a pity perhaps that he hadn't got the names even more mixed up. Something like "Mr Craftysides and Lady Mollie Forbes-Hill".) As for Mollie saying that Liz will be in an asylum by the time she's 50, I should have thought she's in one already – present company of course excepted.

John Russell's[124] translation of Gide's Theseus, printed by the Bodoni Press, Verona, 1949 – did have my name on the title-page, apparently as publisher though I believe that I was only the distributor. Sonia Orwell,[125] when she was working for Horizon, persuaded me to take it on. I seem to remember that it entailed a vast amount of sending out of prospectuses to which there was no great response and that, for years, a stack of copies was subject to flood and burial in the packing room which by now must have finally melted and mouldered. The edition was limited to 200 copies – a nice production, with illustrations by Campigli. Probably it is now v. scarce. I have a copy here (which I would have gladly sold to the

---

121. Leonard Woolf, *The Journey not the Arrival Matters*, Hogarth Press, 1969.

122. Philip Toynbee (1916–81), author and regular book reviewer for *The Observer*.

123. George Weidenfeld (b. 1919), publisher

124. John Russell (b. 1919), author and journalist.

125. Mrs George Orwell (1918–80), described in Hilary Spurling, *Girl from the Fiction Department*, 2002.

Someone – though I suppose lunacy forbids). Your mention of it made me take it down and actually read it. Stylishly translated, it reads as the amusing autobiography of a sh*t.

I BOUGHT the last Leonard Woolf in Aldeburgh – the bookseller there is a wonderfully nice kind man – and enjoyed it deeply, like all the others. The really frightful and beastly review of it was in the TLS. Somehow, the word BLOOMS-BURY seems to be a red rag to a great many people (Liz among them). Do you think that it's because they have an awful feeling that Bloomsbury might be right? I admit that there is what seems a certain arrogance among the Blooms-berries but I think that is only because they are so sure of their conviction and they so hate the sham and the Philistines . . .

1970

*After marrying in 1969, Laura and I spent much of 1970
looking for a house. This contributed to less writing of
letters, as did Heywood and Anne's long trip to America.
Where letters have disappeared, parts of mine can be quoted
from Heywood's letters to Nancy. I have omitted Heywood's
descriptions of events, such as his visit to the health farm
Shrublands, which are described in* The Bookshop at 10
Curzon Street.

H.H.   11/2/70

I suppose that I don't dare ask for Iris Origo's *Giovanna
and Jane* to be cliqued again . . . I remember the mutterings
there used to be about customers who only asked for "difficult" things. I hardly ever buy a new book now . . .

I expect you heard about the awful thing which happened
to Rose[126] [Gathorne-Hardy] about two weeks ago; how she
was crossing a road in Oxford one evening on her way to a
concert with a boy friend when a motor bike ran into the boy
friend and he never recovered consciousness and died the next
morning. She was of course shattered. She came down here
that day and stayed in this house because Antony, her father,
was already here – Ruth is in the Aldeburgh hospital with
some sort of skin trouble. Luckily Lucy was here too – she
and Rose are great friends. Rose decided at first that she
couldn't bear to stay on at Oxford (next term is her last) but
there are rumours that she may have changed her mind.

Anne and I may go to America in the summer as Earl
Evans has asked us to stay. We shall try to let this house and

---

126. Rose Gathorne-Hardy, daughter of Antony and Ruth.

shall not go to the Festival so as to scrape up the fare. Anne hates flying so we shall try to board a freighter.

I hope that by now you have recovered from Christmas . . . Did any of you or them get 'flu? Anne went down on Christmas Eve – just after 8 people had arrived to stay. She had it v. badly and was in bed for two weeks. I was kept busy as nurse and cook . . .

J.S.S. 18/2/70

. . . I was v. upset to hear about Rose. You may have gathered that she appeared at Barbara Robinson's[127] Private View a week ago, to my undisguisable surprise. We had wanted to have her out to Cuddesdon during the weekend preceding, and as she'd been on our minds and hadn't been traced in time, it seemed a trick of Fate that we would then meet [elsewhere] two days later . . .

Don't worry about *Giovanna and Jane*.[128] I've cliqued it regularly for several months, without admitting who'd asked for it, but under the excuse that M[arche]sa Origo had wanted a copy for herself a couple of years ago. It must be rather scarce, and no one wants to part with their copy . . .

Today being Wednesday and last week having been Mollie's week of holiday (mostly spent in a Brighton hotel), I might have a lot to tell you. But Mollie stories have been in rather short supply and not even the presence of a stammering and incompetent accountant (protected by J[eremy] Webster[129]) upset her sufficiently for sparks to fly. And, for

---

127. Barbara Robinson, painter, living near Montpellier, France.
128. It has always been a difficult book to find. Many years later Iris Origo heard that I wanted to reprint it but could not trace a copy. She lent me her only copy, warning me that I would never be forgiven if I lost it.
129. Jeremy Webster, chartered accountant, of Derek Webster's firm in Baker Street.

some reason best known to the Bs, I'm in favour. It appears to date back to the Peak Crisis two days before Christmas when Liz and Setitia both went down with 'flu. In any other job Liz wd. have spent the whole of the previous week in bed: we had to live with a sort of walrus performance of snorting, wheezing and gigantic sneezing, until her temperature soared and she sensibly succumbed. For the first time ever I then witnessed Handy, and occasionally Mollie, really working hard: picking himself up and bracing himself every time another customer appeared, instead of stumbling around at the back of the shop and filling in with a bit of gossip. Meanwhile, at the seat of change, I was almost overwhelmed. But we got through, and then spent the post-Christmas week again without Liz. By the time she came back, the climate was distinctly hostile: my mistakes had been blamed on her, and her 'flu was interpreted as a deliberate blow of selfishness against the establishment. Even I was surprised, though, when Handy made a little speech to me a few days ago just after I'd arrived on a Saturday morning – about how he was "so grateful for the fact that we were getting on so much better together" and that he would like me to convey his thanks to Laura who in his eyes has done a wonderful job of stabilization. L. has still not met Mollie . . .

I've seen Henry briefly, and we are to be allowed by the Bs to have a public lunch together. You might almost think that the Cold War was nearing an end – but it never pays to be smug . . .

H.H. 11/3/70

. . . Thanks so much for your . . . vivid description of the Christmas crisis. There are charitable moments when I feel sorry for Liz, but then one remembers what inflictions she has wrought on one's own sensibilities and that, anyhow, it's all water off a walrus's back, so to speak . . . I am truly glad that you are in favour with the establishment, as it must make shop life much more bearable – though, of course, I can't help missing CMB horror stories . . .

J.S.S.   18/3/70

. . . You may be pleased to hear that my period of favour must now be considered officially over. I hadn't clapped my eyes on Mollie for nearly a fortnight . . ., but she was clearly saving something up for the right moment, and the moment came very early with the appearance of Fortune Stanley. *Thus* [speaking] from behind the partition: "Isn't it incredible how like Faith[130] Fortune is becoming every day? Mollie Robinson[131] was invited over to lunch with Faith and your uncle and she thought they were the *nastiest* couple she'd ever met." Further details followed of what M.R. had said and thought. Well, I kept my peace all day, tho' passing on the gist to everyone downstairs, and waited till 5.20 to [speak] to Handy – saying that I wasn't prepared to vouch for my temper if Mollie ever again passed on malicious gossip about the Ravens. (This may sound pompous, but I think I could guess how Handy would react.) He replied that if anything, he felt as close to the Ravens as I did and what was the gossip? So I told him M's exact words, which I'd noted down, and he tried to wriggle out my suggesting she had said "dottiest couple". I wasn't taking this and, after going very pink, he apologised on her behalf . . . moral victory?? . . .

Did I tell you of Liz's invention of a round-the-titled-family game called Happy Customers? . . . I'm currently working on a board for Bucks and Ladders[132] . . .

130. My aunt Mrs John Raven, Fortune's sister.
131. Mollie Panter-Downes (1906–97), diarist and novelist; married to Clare Robinson.
132. This survives.

H.H. 18/4/70

. . . I hope that CMB has not been making any more such utterly untrue and libellous statements about your relations. I remember talking to John Raven at your wedding and thinking him very nice. It was just before we were going to Skye, where . . . he told me of a walk which I think is the most beautiful I have ever been on.

I am busy learning Italian as hope that, in the autumn, we shall go to stay with Harriet who has now migrated to near Siena. The Italian course, with gramophone records . . . seems a peculiar one. In my lesson this morning was the question "Will the Signorina have a subcutaneous injection of seawater?" They ask these dreadful questions so as to answer them with some dreadful joke (the answer to the above is "No, because I cannot swim" . . .)

We are going to have a very absent year because, in the middle of June, we are meant to be sailing in a freighter to New Orleans . . . It's anxious work about the freighter as cargo comes before passengers and it won't say exactly when it's going until a day or two before and it doesn't seem to be even quite sure that it *is* going to New Orleans and we may be shoved overboard at some terrible place like Miami or Mobile . . . We shall be away for about three months . . .

H.H. 8/8/70 (c/o Dr Earl Evans, Chicago)

I don't know whether it was the effect of being in Chicago in a flat crammed in every room with books from the shop, but last night I had one of the worst Ministry of Fear dreams ever. The shop had transferred itself to a disused tube station. Both platforms were totally blocked by books. However Osbert Sitwell and his secretary managed to fight their way through to give complicated orders while other customers were battling in the background. I was alone on a Saturday

morning except for a brief appearance by Handy with moun-
tains more books which he'd just bought at a sale. He
dumped them down and slid out after scooping some cash
from the booking office. Strong smell of beer. Then Mollie
rang up to say that Osbert's orders had been a practical joke.
Then books began falling on the line and somebody said,
Look out, the line was live . . . However, in spite of these
nightmares, when Earl wrote to Liz today ordering MORE
books, I behaved beautifully and encouraged him and even
sent regards from Anne and me.

We are having the most wonderful and fascinating time.
First, three weeks on a Norwegian cargo boat from Glasgow.
Only 7 other passengers, one of whom – a lone Australian
woman called Bobs – we made great friends with and had
many an off-duty drink with her and the Captain. Then we
called at Charleston and Savannah and were amazed how
many of the old colonial houses there still were. Miami was
horrifying but v. funny. Finally N. Orleans where we went
down Desire St., which the street car went to and walked
round being astounded by those iron balconies, but it was a
temp. of 100° so we didn't stay for more than a night and then
E[arl] drove us 150 miles to a small place on a 30 mile long
beach of white sand where there was marvellous bathing in a
limpid sea until a hurricane called Becky was said by newspaper and TV to be heading straight for us. We had seen acres
of flattened houses from the hurricane of last year called
Camille so it was faintly disturbing as well as exciting. Many
fled but we decided to stick, and it was rather a flop when
next morning it had struck 50 miles away only hurling three
homes into the palm trees. Then there was a 1000 mile drive
to here but as E. has a Cadillac and the roads are fast, it was
easily done in two days – staying a night in Tennessee on the
way.

Chicago at first was a bit sinister. We were told not to walk in the park or through underpasses and on no account in the black quarter but we are toughening up to it and so far have not been mugged (or should it be muggered?) . . . We shall be here till about Aug. 25th. Booked on a boat to Venice on Sept. 9 and then stay with Harriet for two or three weeks. I fear that all this description of long holiday will be mouth-watering for you – hope you're having your autumn share . . .

H.H.   30/10/70

I was pleased to find your CHANGE OF ADDRESS card here and to know that you and Laura have succeeded in establishing yourselves in Islington. Isn't Canonbury Place one of those places with specially nice houses? Even if it isn't, it's a specially nice district. The move must have been frantic and I bet that Curzon St allowed you the minimum time off.[133]

I had been meaning to write to bother you with a tiresome question or two. In my letter from America, did I ask if two books ordered by Earl Evans had been cliqued? They were Iris Origo's *Last Attachment* and R. Gathorne-Hardy's *Logan Pearsall-Smith*. If they were NOT cliqued, don't bother about the latter as I've got copies here and would like to send him one . . .

This long time away has made my memory almost non-existent. We got back here late on Tuesday night – having trained from Florence after our stay with Harriet. Her house is in a most lovely bit of country and it was sunny all the time . . . Rose was there, tutoring the twins [Harriet's step-children], and a tower of strength. It's obviously being the best possible cure for her Oxford tragedy . . .

---

133. Our annual holiday allowance was four weeks, and I took this autumn week as part of it.

I have lent a picture to the Carrington exhibition whose private view is on Thursday next, the 5th. . . . If Handy is going to it, you might diplomatically warn him that Anne and I might be there as you know we might be lending a picture. Oh dear, how I wish that this idiotic hatchet could be buried – but I suppose they will never allow it. . . .

I do hope that one day we shall see you but imagine that you are probably still not quite settled in and that already Gethsemane is casting its dread shadow.

H.H. 2/11/70

So nice to get your very fascinating letter [lost]. This is just to say that it would be fine if we could fix a preliminary drink before Carrington party next Thurs. The thing is WHERE. [A pub in Davies street was suggested; if it had recently foundered, he would wait in the bar at Claridge's but he was "frightened of the economics" and feared that we'd be spotted by a Buchanan ally. In the end we met at the party, not beforehand.]

Anne's niece, Tina Letanka, the one who married a black doctor, has just written to say that one of her husband's patients wants a set of Addison's works and she asks how to find one. Is he just The Spectator? Tell me on Thurs. . . .

Heywood gave a graphic account of this party to Nancy Mitford (see The Bookshop at 10 Curzon Street, *page 149). I remember it best because my overcoat was "borrowed" by Raymond Mortimer. He left behind his own scruffy coat which I collected from the Grosvenor Gallery and exchanged by taking it 100 yards across Canonbury Place to the house he shared with his architect partner Paul Hyslop and, at a later date, Jack Lander. This led to my getting to know them, and thereafter I delivered books to them regularly.*

J.S.S.   11/70
[quoted from H.H.'s letter to Nancy Mitford of 25/11/70]

When Mollie came in on Friday morning, she had that look in her eye which bodes ill for all. HER stationery cupboard was said to be in a frightful mess. It's true that I've been ordering stationery for the shop *faute de mieux*, and there are better things to do than dust out the cupboard once a week. Everyone knows where things are anyway. But on this occasion an ink bottle, Handy's ink bottle, was on its side. Anyone else would have stood it up again. Mollie did no such thing. She caught me on my way to the packing room with "This is in a disgusting state, etc." to which I said that we had been exceedingly busy. I then went upstairs again. She followed a minute or two later, and as she prepared to sit down again (Liz was downstairs) came out with: "The trouble with you is that you're going to want to retire from the shop before Handy does. I've never heard anyone grumble so much about his work."

"Balls."

"What about that stationery cupboard then?"

"Perhaps you would like to look after the stationery cupboard, then?"

"No I would not. The trouble with you is that you won't pay any interest to the other side of the shop. You are quite good with the books but you won't look after anything else. As to being able to run it, you'd just never do it."

"Balls."

I was then determined to get in my side of the story to Standaside while she was under her Friday dryer. He was just feeble: "Mollie works hard, we all work hard, I work hard." He also said that I shouldn't have spoken like that to a Lady; I did not produce the obvious retort.

There are no surviving letters until the end of September,
with the exception of a postcard from Heywood in March
asking if the shop could turn up a copy of a 1931 booklet
on rum by H. Warner Allen. At the same time he wanted
to know, on Anne's behalf, a fair price for her to give for a
second-hand set of the Dictionary of National Biography.
No answer survives.

This lacuna prompted me to look at my own bookshelves
to remind myself of some of the books in the previous five
years that I had pushed in the shop and for which I now
had some faithful customers. They included John Julius
Norwich's two volumes on Sicily, David Cecil's Visionary
and Dreamer, *Solzhenitsyn's* First Circle *and James Morris's*
Pax Britannica. *I had to fight hard over the last because*
Handy disapproved of such brilliantly colourful history.
He preferred solid military stuff and, with an audible curl
of his lip, would describe James Morris as "John's sort
of historian", implying that he was neither serious nor
academically sound. Several of "my" books were written by
old friends of the shop, such as Osbert Lancaster's With an
Eye to the Future, *James Lees-Milne's* Another Self *and Iris*
Origo's Images and Shadows. *There were also signs that*
some of my own generation, from Piers Paul Read to Mark
Girouard, would start to contribute to Heywood Hill's
bestsellers.

This still did not mean that anyone but Handy ordered
our new books but the publishers' reps had started to realize
what books I might enjoy and, where possible, they would
provide proof copies. In late 1970 John Julius Norwich had
told me about his first "Christmas Cracker", of which he had

*printed two hundred copies for his friends. I asked if I could
look at it overnight and then asked how many we could have
to sell. The answer was fifty and, priced at ten shillings, they
rapidly sold out.*

H.H. 25/9/71

If Kenneth Sinclair-Loutit[134] is still a shop customer and
"on the books", could you possibly let me have his address?
I'd be v. grateful. Lucy and family are going to Morocco next
week and I'd like her to have the address – just in case any
calamity might befall them.

How are you and how is Laura? Is there any baby news
yet? . . . [Our first child Joseph William was born on 29 September.]

J.S.S. 2/10/71

Many thanks for your letter of greeting. I'm feeling
extremely conscientious about replying to letters as Laura
doesn't have a minute to spare at Charing X [Hospital] . . .

It's difficult to resume on so long a period at the shop and I
try not to keep turning over old problems or resentments for
fear of catching Dibuckilitis. [Complaints followed about a
salary rise which had been promised in September. The shop
had had its best figures ever with a turnover of £143,000, but
Handy claimed that he had been responsible for a large proportion because Alistair McAlpine had spent £36,000 on
flower and bird books] . . . The contract[135] is a maddening
document because it's so out of proportion with my responsi-

---

134. Dr Kenneth Sinclair-Loutit, who worked for the World Health
Organisation, was the father of Nicky, Jonny Gathorne-Hardy's second
wife.
135. The contract dated from 1968 and did not allow for inflation or for
any change in my circumstances.

bilities in the shop and the prices nowadays, but, as Handy pointed out when I became a bit shirty, my case wouldn't stand up in a court of law . . .

Liz has never entered this particular arena because she has no contract . . . She is not as indigent as she always appeared . . . because she's now established as the F.T.'s third operatic reviewer. This meant that she was given an almost free holiday in Salzburg and means that there's not an evening she misses at the Garden, Coliseum or suitable rendezvous in the provinces. She's off to Edinburgh and Glasgow next weekend, and it won't be long before she launches off to Wexford. This is splendid from the point of view of her future career, when she leaves no. 10, but it's not much fun for anyone – The shop has been incredibly busy throughout the summer and Liz had no holiday to restore her fund of energy. She was v. unpopular during the Postal Strike because she did so little, and the Bs can hardly bear it whenever I am away. It was a change to return from holiday and to find that one was welcome, if only as a Buffer State . . . We had spent two weeks in Cornwall and Somerset and the weather had been evil . . . so to pass the time when the rain came down, I'd sought out such bookshops as I could find . . . All in all, I bought about £500 worth of books and they all sold immediately. Was I offered any expenses? No. Should I have claimed them? Yes, I suppose I should. When I did in late August, Handy said that no one had asked me to get books on my holiday and that was my look-out. Meanwhile Henry has bought his second new car as a shop expense, and Handy has offered me a year's travel allowance of £20.

When I came back to the shop [after the baby's birth], I found Liz and Handy acting out an "armed neutrality". Setitia, still our secretary, realized late on Wed. that she hadn't typed out the Clique list for me and suggested that I would not be extra-pleased. Liz [said] "Don't you dare apologise to

John tomorrow, you can perfectly well do it for him tomorrow morning – attack is by far the best form of defence" . . . Don't imagine, as one of my gossipy aunts did, that I'm not on speaking terms with the Bs, indeed I've been invited to Castle B. for Sunday lunch tomorrow . . . if I go down with the Gripes, it will be certain witchcraft . . .

H.H.   15/11/71

. . . very interested by your letter but also fairly appalled by the niggardly way the shop has been treating you. . . . I remember how, in my own small way, I used to do a great deal of the so necessary hack work without ever so much as a thank you and how no iota of interest was shown in the books and objects which I used to buy – although they usually sold very well. . . .

Now comes this extraordinary news which I received last week in a letter from Henry. Bacon![136] I pray that it is not going to affect you in any adverse way and that the resulting hurricanes have not been too appalling. He said that "under the guise of friendship" more and more had been engineered to "undermine his position" and that Handy's line had been "You'll never find a better moment to get out than now." However, I expect that there is another side to it and it did sound as if Henry's action had been a bit abrupt – to put it mildly. I long to know what you feel about it all . . .

J.S.S.   19/11/71

. . . Your letter arrived the morning after I'd had a drink with Henry at White's. He wanted to tell me his side of the

---

136. David Bacon (b. 1933), chartered accountant. He owned the bookshop from this date until 1991 when it was bought by a group of shareholders, with the Duke of Devonshire holding the majority.

HH sale and his theories about my prospects. He managed to bring out all my most puritanical inclinations. He was playing Slosh[137] with Lord Scarbrough[138] when I arrived and they naturally preferred to finish their game. They both looked fairly dissolute: I was reminded of the characters in *The Way we Live Now* who devote their time, energy and money to wasting all three. They were so frightfully bad at the game that it took a further 20 minutes for Lord S. to reach 100, at which point Henry handed over £5 . . . I was reminded of our weekend at Duncton when we were shown the clothes Henry had provided for his children's Guy – all in very good wearable condition and including a silk tie that he'd bought and not specially fancied.

. . . As regards the shop, I'd be the first to acknowledge Henry's charm, and he's always been decent to me. While he's owned the business, he hasn't ruined it and he's certainly had to put up with some rough treatment from Handy. Of course no two characters *could* be more opposite and it was never likely there'd be much sympathy. But really Henry is too hopeless by half, feckless, irresponsible and not averse to a bit of sharp practice . . . He didn't tell me how much Mr Bacon is paying him but it sounds as if he's made a considerable profit on what he paid you.[139] He's had an income every year (which he thought measly), a car and its running expenses gratis, and all his books for free. What has he contributed? NOTHING . . .

Here endeth the lesson. Steam has been let off.

What about the new owner . . . He works very hard, he understands business and he's been my customer, making

---

137. A form of billiards in which each coloured ball scores differently.
138. The Earl of Scarbrough, "Dickon" (1932–2004), an Eton
contemporary of Henry Vyner and a business acquaintance of David Bacon.
139. This was "one of the only profitable business deals Henry ever
achieved". I later heard that the selling price had been £75,000.

small-ish collections of authors that he likes. He believes in the shop's staying exactly as it is now . . . where A. McAlpine wanted to scrap the print-room and children's room, and turn the whole of downstairs into a wonderful antiquarian book gallery.

This week's prize remark, unheard by me but reported back, was made by your friend Adrian Daintrey[140] at the party to launch Joan Haslip's new book.[141] "Of course Heywood is the only person in the world about whom one couldn't be nasty." This was addressed to Mollie . . .

H.H. 6/12/71

. . . I am so glad that Bacon is *YOUR* customer and I do hope he will do better for you than slippery Henry V.

I can't write a proper letter now as am stuck in bed with 'flu while Anne is stuck downstairs in her crippled state [she had fallen in early October and had spent four weeks in an Ipswich nursing home] and we can communicate only by telephone. Luckily Lucy has come to the rescue and is the unfortunate go-between. . . .

I dreamed last night that Viva King[142] had taken me to some v. odd Gala "do" at Cov. Garden. One sat on bar stools by the orchestra rail and was given dubious drinks. The unknown woman next to me said "There is Liz in a beautiful dress." I looked but fear that the effect was hideous. It was all-white. An embarrassing evening . . .

---

140. Adrian Daintrey (1902–88), portrait painter and illustrator.
141. Joan Haslip, *Imperial Adventurer: Emperor Maximilian and his Empress.*
142. Viva King (1893–1979), author of *The Weeping and the Laughter.*

1972

H.H.   13/2/72

I was touched and delighted by the so welcome last Edel vol[143] from Buck and Bacon – not to mention their "respectful wishes" [This was a duplicated advance copy sent by Hart-Davis by mistake]. I shall take it to Italy when we go to visit Harriet in April . . .

Here we trip quaintly with rushlight and taper.[144] I imagine that, in Curzon St., there is a hissing hurricane lamp (just to add to all the other hissings and hurricanes). Actually all that has happened to us as yet are two blackouts last Friday lasting about two hours each, but as the whole house is run entirely by electricity, cooking and heating – we have been buying fat church candles and hopeless little oil cookers (Anne has already had one disaster through overfilling the little rotter and causing a paraffin flood in the kitchen).

Peggy Clutten[145] asked John [Hill] to go and criticize her paintings . . . I fear that he felt very critical indeed though suppressed it to the best of his ability . . . Why I tell you this is because Peggy told John that she had gone to London to a party given for one of her old school pupils and mistresses where a large woman came up to her and said "Hullo Peggy." Peggy said "I don't think I know you." She was C.M.B. Peggy hadn't recognized her. I'm sorry to say that gave mild pleasure to some . . .

---

143. Leon Edel's final volume of his life of Henry James, *The Master*.

144. The three-day week had imposed constraints in all quarters.

145. Peggy Clutten, who lived in Aldeburgh, had previously owned a school in Notting Hill patronised by Hills and Gathorne-Hardys. By coincidence, she had been a close friend of one of my aunts, Mary Raven.

J.S.S.   15/2/72

I've been feeling hyper-browned off with HH for the last few days and it was v. nice to have such a cheerful letter from you. Handy retired to bed last Friday, just as our power was first cut, with the deepest, gloomiest forebodings of his health. He recovered next morning, but of course I had to stand in (Setitia is also down with 'flu) – and then up went his temperature with Mollie's return from a week in Brighton, and bang went my arranged plan for yesterday, which had taken 6 full months to hatch, to see and value Mrs P[atrick] Gibson's[146] books in Groombridge. I'm not sure if she bought books from you. She's the most book-minded of Mrs Pearson's[147] daughters and she's got an incredible collection of Pre-Raph. pictures. (Her husband's now Chairman of the Arts Council, as well as the tycoon who took over Longmans and then Penguin.) She's very nice and couldn't have been more sympathetic about my cancelling everything at the 11th hour . . .

I have a story which will not find its way into H.B.'s memoirs. A letter arrives from Lady Jones [Enid Bagnold][148] a fortnight ago. She has just been doing up a flat for her son in Hamilton Terrace and she desperately needs 200 books to fill gaping empty shelves. What can we do? Handy has just bought some rubbish from Lady West and he sees this as a golden chance. "The hour brings forth the man" etc. So I run around the shelves madly calculating how much we could charge for 200 books and come up with a figure of £70. Handy then writes a superbly ingratiating letter to the effect

---

146. Lady Gibson, whose husband was later Chairman of the National Trust.

147. Mrs Alicia Pearson of Parham Park, Sussex; collector and bibliophile.

148. Enid Bagnold (1889–1981), author of *National Velvet*, whose autobiography had been published in 1969.

that she'd be awfully lucky to get them at this price, that he'd known someone extremely well who'd known her x years ago and that he was Yours sincerely, Handasyde Buchanan. Three or four days pass and we wonder what to do with Lady West's rubbish which is sitting by the door looking dreary. On Sat. morning, when Handy has withdrawn from the fray, he rings up to organize what he can against power-cuts (which is nil) and speaks to Liz: "Is there any post for me?" "Oh, the post's only just come . . . Oh yes, here we are (slight giggle) but this is addressed to Miss Handasyde Buchanan." She opens it and looks for the sender's name, none other than Lady Jones. Dear Miss Buchanan, it went, I'm afraid my son went into a Brighton bookshop without my knowing and [they] offered him 200 books for £10. I'm sure your books would be much gayer . . . Now how long has Enid Bagnold been a customer? How long have her sons been customers? Quite a long time, long enough surely for them all to have learned either a) that the driving force in the shop was a spinster lady or b) that E.H.B. in all his famous roles has been a transvestite.

I had a long talk with Mr Bacon a fortnight ago and told him a few home truths. . . . He naturally doesn't want the shop to be shipwrecked by the Bs . . . and he's now a bit better prepared for the sort of hurricanes and hissings we know so well.

Heywood's next letter, dated 15 March, enclosed a postcard from the Dowager Countess of Glasgow, Anne's aunt. She asked if his bookshop might trace a 1962 book called The Heretic Pharaoh *but "I can't help feeling that a word from you might do wonders!" Heywood speculated on what a word from him might have brought about and hoped the card might make me shriek.*

He and Anne had been burying an aunt near Luton. A memorial service had been held near Harting in Sussex to which Heywood had gone with his sister Sheila. Staying the night with a cousin, he was "suddenly astounded by a man called Rowley[149] saying that he owned the building of no. 10. He was only there for a drink so I didn't have much chance of talking to him or finding out what he is really like."

H.H.   17/5/72

I was interested about Michael Lichnowsky, and I wonder what he is like as an old man. I have a neurotic feel that the shop Furies keep a lot from me. When young, Lichnowsky was like a furious firework. Ralph Jarvis[150] and I knew him at Cambridge and we had the most extraordinary sort of Ruritanian holiday when he asked us to stay with his parents in their German palace. A full orchestra used to play during dinner. He had an equally explosive sister called Lenni and I wonder what happened to her. His father was the German ambassador in London when the 1914 war started and his red-haired mother used to go for rides on the open tops of London buses. So do try and write a little line not too far anon.

. . . Staying with Harriet in Italy . . ., we had lunch with Harold Acton who told me that E.H.B. had damned his short stories.[151] I must say they don't seem to me to be v.g., though I was rather fascinated by one called AN OLD SCHOOL PAL about someone who was also an old school pal of mine and, to our dismay, has bought himself a cottage in this village.[152]

---

149. Sir Charles Rowley (b. 1926), who is still the shop's landlord.
150. Ralph Jarvis, cousin of Anne Hill, Cambridge contemporary of Heywood, and father of Lady Cranbrook.
151. *Tit for Tat*, published by Hamish Hamilton, 1972.
152. Jim Knapp-Fisher, who at one time worked for Sidgwick and Jackson, publishers.

J.S.S.   28/5/72

Anon has proved longer than it should have been . . .

First, your friend Count Lichnowsky. If only he'd approached me and not Handy. What could have been worse than "I'd like to see Mr Heywood Hill, I haven't seen him for 35 years." Answered, v. gruffly, with "Mr Hill hasn't worked here for ten years." Then:

C.L.: Well, do tell me about him, what he's doing and so on.

H.B. He lives in the country and he has Nothing to do with the shop.

C.L. Well, is he married?

H.B. He's been married for more than 30 years.

C.L. Has he children?

H.B. He has two daughters and they're both married as well.

C.L. Well, perhaps I'd better leave a note for him and you could tell him that I've been to visit him.

H.B. (very grudgingly letting him come to the back of the shop) You'd better leave the card here (on Liz's desk).

C.L. Did you know another friend of mine called Ralph Jarvis?

H.B. Yes, I think he's dead now.

J.S.S. No surely, Handy, you're wrong. He's alive as far as I know.

C.L. Well, what about him? Is he married?

H.B. (getting more testy every minute) Yes, he's been married for more than 30 years.

So he left, having discovered the barest minimum and having given no clue where he was staying or for how long. The impression he left with me . . . was that he had a pretty thick skin (tho' he may be used to dusty receptions in Brazil) and a fairly disagreeable appearance – sleek, running to paunch, with enormous plastic-looking ears.

My comments followed on Jonny Gathorne-Hardy's[153] Rise and Fall of the English Nanny, which I'd read in proof, and found "riddled with mistakes" and in need of some proper sub-editing. It contained a page devoted to an anecdote, told on two separate occasions, concerning Handy and his lifelong interest in bottoms – derived from a precocious sight of his nanny undressing.

Prize Mollie-ism for May. She came in on Friday morning when Handy was having his lunch and said to Liz and me: "Handy rang me up as soon as he got to the shop this morning and said that he hated starting the day with a row and really I had been a bit cross when he left. Well, I said I didn't know what he'd been talking about, as far as I knew, I'd just been my usual self, you know what I mean; I didn't think that I'd been cross at all, I may have been in another room and not paying attention to what he was saying . . ."

The Bs are at Witherslack this weekend. It wouldn't surprise me if Mollie never went there again: she was shaping up for a super-row with Fortune [Stanley], and F. only has her on sufferance. Setitia had a dream about three weeks ago that Mollie had volunteered to stay behind because she couldn't face it, and Setitia went instead. The dream was very coherent. Setitia was given a very chilly reception at the Stanleys and was put at the children's table with the Stanley boys.

When she was getting into her best country house style, Mollie came out with "We don't seem to have many of the real aristocrats as customers nowadays. Andrew Devonshire's

---

153. Jonathan Gathorne-Hardy (b. 1933), novelist and biographer, who had worked briefly in the shop several years earlier.

one of the only ones who's been faithful to us." Liz surprisingly said it was no bad thing that we didn't just think about titles. It was a jibe at [me] who hasn't been to Chatsworth for a weekend. There'll be many worse jibes to come because the pace is hotting up to have her removed for ever – April the deadline. You will say you've heard all this before . . .

Heywood's letter of 28 May listed a collection of old books "none of them in marvellous condition", which had been offered to him by a "rather amusing eccentric" in Aldeburgh. He didn't think they were worth a SPECIAL effort, but suggested that we came over from Dedham and had a look.

He was just finishing Leon Edel's last volume of Henry James. "Did you notice this bit – talking about the visit to Lamb House of H.J.'s nephew:–

The lesson he carried away from his elderly uncle was the memory of hearing him say that 'three things in life are important. The first is to be kind. The second is to be kind. The third is to be kind . . .'

I don't believe that that lesson would be carried away from Curzon St. – what?"

J.S.S.   3/10/72

. . . I hope you cannot imagine what a frightful time we've been having at no. 10. Did you hear of Mr Stafford's death? On holiday, with Margot and his children, at Thorpe Ness. He had taken a chalet, and after 10 days he had a heart attack and died, pff! Like that. There was an inquest which didn't prove anything conclusive . . . The funeral was in Catford, organized by Mr S's brothers. Handy and Lady B went down to it in a hired car, and the shop sent a magnificent Moyses Stevens wreath, *no* expense spared . . .

Very fortunately, Mr S had arranged for a mate of his called J. McMahon to work in the evenings while he was on holiday, and he (J.McM.) was persuaded to stay on as our packer once he'd given in his notice to Oppenheims [book-shop near South Kensington underground station]. He's had about as rough an introduction as anyone could have, and he's stood up to it reasonably well. The shop has been *fiendishly* busy . . . Apart from the perennial problems of abrasiveness, there hasn't been more than a day or two since June when we haven't had one person away . . . Handy is worried about the long-term future and feels a conscience about my being left in the shit . . . Both the Bs are almost inclined to hark back to the halcyon days of Henry . . . at least, they say, he was a gentleman and he did understand . . .

[Gossip about the likely Christmas sellers: the second volumes of Quentin Bell's *Virginia Woolf* and Elizabeth Long-ford's *Wellington*; Cecil Woodham-Smith's *Queen Victoria*; Solzhenitsyn's *August 1914*.] Why are there no decent English novels? All the young novelists produce such grim, humour-less stuff on the boring state of their own psyche, e.g. David Storey's *Pasmore*, which will no doubt be praised for its earthy, no-nonsense realism. Perhaps I should leave Curzon-strasse and write a runaway best seller called *The Shop* . . .

H.H.   8/10/72

I was shocked by the news of Mr S's death. Very sad. Shocked too, in another way, [that life] seemed to have turned sour . . . If only it could go back to what it was in the begin-ning and be run by Anne and me and you and Laura. I'm sure we would not have subjected ourselves to those heaving under-currents or depressing over-currents. If you can stay on, you could restore it to more like it used to be . . . I some-times think that perhaps the new books are a CURSE and that it should be turned into a smaller calmer business of second-hand books only . . .

Heywood's letter of 22 October, hand-written, thanked me for sending him the second volume of Virginia Woolf *which he was reading on a ten-day jaunt in the West Country. Anne and he were staying with Harriet's parents-in-law at Culham Court, near Henley-on-Thames. Anne had been assaulted by "a wolfhound, the size of a pony", on arrival but it hadn't caused more than a scratch "and we are all pretending that it was a friendly gesture". It was "rather enjoyable sinking into luxury for a short space before returning to Snape with a bump tomorrow".*

1973

Writing to Nancy Mitford on 24 February, Heywood
paraphrased the latest news from the shop: "I gather that
great boilings have been going on. The new owner has
got a new woman instead of Mollie. The new woman[154]
has enormous thighs and short skirts so Handy must be in a
delirium. He is said to have been heard to say to her, 'I should
never have married Mollie.' He is also said to get terrible
wiggings when he goes home in the evening. Liz is said to
be leaving. All this may be just gossip – so don't breathe too
many words."

J.S.S.   24/2/73

Did you notice a particularly sinister quality about the
storm that broke over London at 5.30 yesterday? Those who
had seen the traumas of the working day at no. 10 were sure
that it was instigated by their resident Witch . . .

Mollie had been looking after Handy – suffering from
gastric 'flu – on Thursday while she finished the last stages of
her Christmas bills. She arrived yesterday morning spoiling
for trouble: Handy was out of the shop and she wanted to
have a real go at Mrs Potter. She was much encouraged in this
by Liz, who has been nearly as foul to Mrs P. as her mentor.
She had a minor row immediately and Mrs P answered back
tartly and effectively. She drew her weapons together and
descended for the full broadside. "My ledgers are this, and
you don't understand that," etc. riposted by "They're not
your ledgers, they are the shop ledgers, and you're only upset
because Mr Bacon has asked you to retire early." Well, who

---

154. Mrs Potter, the new book-keeper, who was to take over Mollie's job.

has ever dared to say that before? Mollie went over the edge: "You're totally unsuitable for this shop and you are a SMALL MINDED little woman." Exit up the stairs to explain to the rest of us who have smelt the brimstone: "The row had to come sometime and it's a good thing it's come so soon." She was in a very bad state and her mouth had that awful, dry, cracking sound that has always meant Trouble. Meanwhile, exit Mrs P. to 3 Queen Street,[155] looking very tough. The telephone rings and Mr Bacon asks me to come round and see him immediately. He sits me down and tells me that he has had enough nastiness from Mollie, and that this was the last day that he would employ her. No question of going back, she was getting the sack for ever – no bills, no voluntary helping Mrs P., nothing. Would I face the circumstances? he asked [assuming that Handy would resign]. Not much option really but I assured him that H. would *never* leave as a result of all this.

Mollie had her hair done, as usual, and after a weep somewhere unspecified, she went back to no. 10 and rang up Handy. He was angry and told her she must go round to Queen St. and eat humble pie. She was prepared to do this but she was shaking with fear. Ten minutes later she was back in the shop, saying that she had been sacked for ever. Goodbye, goodbye, I shall now go back to Handy.

Half an hour passes and Mr Bacon appears. He passes me in the front of the shop and, most unadvisedly, announces the news to Liz. Liz has been very shaken by Mollie's dismissal and has been trying to persuade Setitia to hand in her resignation (with Liz) forthwith. So Mr B. gets a torrent of anti-Mrs P. abuse – the first he's heard from Liz – and a conditional, and strongly emotional, offer to give in her notice. The torrent continued unabated for 10 minutes at

155. David Bacon's office.

fullest Forbesian volume while I served a couple of customers (it was like being in front of the footlights and hearing the main lead having a nervous breakdown ten feet away). Mr B. stuck it out and the notice was retracted – for how long?

We will now see how Handy survives with the least suffering to himself. Of all of us, he has had far the rawest deal. At least we can get away from the poison. If he happened to get so drunk one evening that he took a carving knife to Mollie, I would cheerfully go into the witness box and testify to his innocence. Wouldn't you? . . .

H.H. 12/3/73 (from Tuscany)

Your news, forwarded by Anne, was totally electrifying. After absorbing it myself, I read it out loud to Harriet and Tim who were equally (no, not *quite* equally – not having suffered from the sorcery in the way that I have) riveted. Anyway, they were thoroughly infected by my electrocution and we all went up to the village shop and drank a bottle of Asti Spumanti (the nearest we could get to champers). I do feel a bit sorry for Handy – though, goodness, he brought it on himself. I've just remembered how, when he told me he was going to marry Mollie, he said "I ought not to be doing it" (meaning deserting his first wife), as well as how he and M. would never combine against me, which is of course what they did . . .

Do beware of poison, which I'm sure will still be brewed in Earls Court. In fact, a potion has already reached me. On the afternoon after the day of rejoicing, I fell down while on a walk and cracked my ankle, so I'm now in plaster up to the knee and immobilised.

I LONG, of course, to have news of the aftermath. All H's art of dodgery must be employed – even to the extent of appeasing Mr Bacon and Mrs P. (what a brave Amazon she must be) and perhaps staging a come-back for M. . . . Is there really no danger of that? And Liz? . . .

I sometimes wonder if an alliance with John Sandoe might not be an idea. He is so extremely efficient at the new side that he might be a substitute for Liz and take a large burden off your shoulders and let you concentrate on the old . . .

P.S. One of those real hopeless customer questions from a neighbour here. A book about a man in California who kept wolves as Alsatians. She had it in paperback but lost it, she found it such a help with her jackal.

J.S.S. 21/3/73

. . . I'd been looking forward to [describing] the aftermath . . . but I feel totally drained after a hectic afternoon at Stanford Dingley.[156] The whole operation has been fraught with ghastly traps – mainly because I'm so bad at telling white lies – and I opted to drive down in our little car (the presence of which Handy has not been told about) and to pick up such books as would be good for our stock. If I'd had a full day, the results would *probably* have been the same but I was working at breakneck speed – and of course there's a terrific lot of work waiting for me tomorrow. Of course, I'm delighted to have been given the chance to buy some books before Sotheby's and I'll try to make my offer *very* generous.

The best I can do on the HH score is to jot down some remarks that I've heard.

Mr Bacon: I have put up with quite enough by now. She has simply treated me like a naughty boy who has stolen fruit (this was because Mollie had prevented any cheques being signed by Mr B. while Handy was ill). It's an insult to my

---

156. Bob Gathorne-Hardy's mill house, where I'd been asked to advise and make an offer for suitable HH books, my first such commission.

pride and I'm not going to take any more of it. (Last Wednesday, two days after returning from Brighton, Mollie came to the shop at midday "to get her wages". The reactions were predictable. Liz was all over her, darling Mollie, etc.; Handy was somewhat upset; Mrs P. was out of sight; and I, having just had lunch with Jonny [Gathorne-Hardy] registered a facial expression that Setitia said could never be repeated.)

Setitia: I had never believed you when you said there was something between Liz and Mollie, but I do now. Liz has been AWFUL ever since Mrs P. arrived . . .

Liz (this morning): I'm hours behind with my work because I had that fiend sitting opposite me for half the morning . . .

Handy (on being told by Setitia, jokingly, that she felt like putting her head in a gas oven but that wouldn't be much use because the gas had been cut off): Will you please not make remarks like that. You're the second person who has said that to me today and the first person meant it seriously.

Mollie (during her reappearance): I'm just off to Hardy Amies[157] to collect my suit and then I thought I'd fit in a nice exhibition – I'm *so* busy now in my retirement . . .

Actually M. has NOTHING to do. She has cut herself off from all her friends, she doesn't like books, she has no work to do in her flat (though the towels are probably changed every day instead of every week) and her relatives must have evolved an effective scheme to keep her at bay. You should be pleased that you have been demoted from your position as Enemy No. 1: she apparently still wakes up in the middle of the night shouting imprecations at Mr Bacon.

The future, oh! the future. It's so frantic keeping abreast with the work that I never have a moment to meditate . . . I'm

---

157. Sir Hardy Amies (1909–2003), couturier and loyal customer.

not v. happy about the idea of John Sandoe and feel I must somehow see HH to a Happy Future . . .

H.H.   3/4/73

. . . I'm so glad that Anne got you down to S. Dingley, but sorry that it was such a rush. I feel sure that there are all sorts of buried treasure there which would need a lot of digging to discover. However – I hope you're pleased with what you got. The family are pleased with your price and Anne was impressed by your speed. . . .

The strange thing is that, maddeningly, I used to dream much too often – say twice a week – of the Witch but ever since Sack-day I haven't had one at all. . . .

Anne says that you were longing for [Bob Gathorne-Hardy's] Rossetti collection[158] but were v. controlled and good about it saying that perhaps it ought to go to Sotheby's.

J.S.S.   3/6/73

The situation at no. 10 gets more complicated every week. Less than three weeks ago, Handy, for once precipitate, interviewed and decided on a new recruit, suggested by the Oxford Appointments Board. His name is Mark Wormald; a Colleger at Eton, read Greats at Magdalen, got a Third (shades of EHB) and spent three months last year working at Mowbrays in Cambridge. He started work last Tuesday and I rather like him. Ghastly for him, of course, to join such a

---

158. Bob Gathorne-Hardy (1902–73), had made a fine collection of Christina Rossetti. He also had most of Jane Austen in first edition. These were on a bottom shelf and had many years' worth of dust on their top edges, with the exception of *Pride and Prejudice*. I asked the young cleaning lady why this was so and was told that that volume had been lent to her when she had been watching the TV version. She was dumbstruck when I told her their value.

mad-house but I think he might fit in. He will have his summer holiday at the same time as the Bs: Handy wants to protect him from the wolves, or perhaps the chief she-wolf.

So it looked as if, at last, we were going to have enough hands to cope with the work. Then on Tuesday morning, straight after the Bank Hol., Mrs Potter gave in her notice. She's found a v. good job with a firm in Dover St., and leaves on June 15th.

No, we are NOT having Mollie back. Mr Bacon won't have her at any price – but who will come instead? While the Bs are away, Websters[159] are being recalled. And who did the recalling? Not Handy, not Mr Bacon, but Mollie . . .

H.H.   6/6/73

Your newsletters never fail to make me gasp. I shan't be at all surprised if one day soon you write and tell me that [Mollie] has cast a spell on Mr Bacon so that he sacks himself – like Henry – and finds some poor sap to buy the place and reinstate her. However, she hasn't YET reappeared in my dreams . . .

Our second son George was born on 15 June and my next letter gave Heywood the news. I went on: "Handy's away (in Beynac), and Liz looks as if she's had an hour's sleep in the last fortnight. It's lucky she doesn't have two small boys to stop her enjoying that hour . . . On the day before the Buck holiday, CMB arrived to collect her wages, Triumphant of course because Mrs Potter had just left. For quarter of an hour she and Liz tore the benighted lady limb from limb – a real ORGY of malice – while Setitia was forced to listen. When they had finished, Mollie put her hand on Liz's

---

159. Our auditors were Derek Webster & Co.; see note 129.

shoulder and, with the blackest of black looks towards Setitia, said "You've been so loyal to me, dear Liz . . ."

Five minutes later, when I'd come back from Sotheby's, she asked what we were going to call the baby (Joseph's name had been greeted with "Those Jewish names have become rather fashionable these days, haven't they?") When I told her, there was a marvellous pregnant pause of 15 seconds when her brain was working at triple tempo for something unpleasant to produce. The unpleasantness failed to emerge because Handy came in with "it's a very good name . . ." and all she could think of was that a lot of kings had names like that.

H.H.   25/6/73

Could you some time very kindly answer a v. boring question? I have had a letter from my Cornish aunt [at Trewithen] from which I quote:

Many years ago George[160] bought two sets, 3 vols. each, of Flora and Sylva, 1903. They are beautifully illustrated and the paper is that lovely thick paper with rough edges and the books are bound in green cloth. Unfortunately the second set was in the bookcase near his armchair at the bottom and his Dachshund found that a mouse had got behind the books and he chewed the bottom of the spines of the two volumes which has not improved the look of them. However, the books themselves and the rest of the bindings are quite all right. I know someone who would like to buy them, so could you give me an idea of their value (the second set with damaged spines).

I remember that, in my day, I used to groan whenever Flora and Sylva was mentioned. All classy gardeners had it

---

160. Elizabeth Johnstone's father.

and they all thought it was very valuable – but it WASN'T. It was a drug. But as I am so rusty and prices have changed, I daren't say that to auntie. Don't bother about the mouse.

Yesterday I met Pamela Onslow who was staying in Aldeburgh for a bit of the Festival. I asked her how her daughter is – the one who worked in the shop and married Bron.[161] After saying that the daughter had been v. upset by the death of her mother-in-law, she asked "Is that odd little man who used to be in the shop still there?" I was rather surprised as I am generally told by people how they adore that sweet little Mr B. P.O. went on to say "I have never heard such a name-dropper in all my life. Evelyn this and Evelyn that." I told her that I thought that trait had been rather encouraged by his wife, whose father had been Mayor of King's Lynn and so used to meet the Queen Mother when she popped over from Sandringham. That somehow seemed to make P.O. SHRIEK with laughter. All rather balm to me, I'm ashamed to say.

J.S.S.   28/6/73

. . . Yes, Flora and Sylva is a real drug (how did that expression start?) but a set in good condition is *sold* now for £20–£25. We've got a set on an upper shelf for £25 and it'll probably stay there for a long time . . .

I loved the P. Onslow story. We are going to have an autumn dedicated to E. Waugh and How I Knew Him So Well.[162] Even now I can almost recite Handy's record word for word.

---

161. Teresa, daughter of Lady Onslow (1915–92), had married Evelyn Waugh's son Auberon. In the 1990s I met her at a *Spectator* party and told her some of my memories of Mollie. She was incredulous.
162. Handy had written a chapter in David Pryce-Jones's *Evelyn Waugh and his World.*

In a postcard thanking me for having found Iris Origo's
Leopardi *for £3, Heywood wrote "You are immensely*
tantalising about 'abundant news',," but the letter has been
lost. A week later, he reported that Anne had broken her
ankle and that they were driving to Italy to stay with Harriet
for about a month. His "charitable thoughts about the witch
are not lasting".

H.H.   2/11/73

[Comments and criticism of Piers Paul Read's *A Married Man* which I thought he'd enjoy; one of the main characters seemed to resemble Henry Vyner.] My room is a deep morass of old letters as I try to search out those from Nancy.[163] I am supposed to be seeing Harold Acton on 12th or 13th. Countess [Mollie] is certain to slip in first but I feel she'll always win whatever happens – she's such a proficient poisoner. . . . Anne has written to Jim Lees-Milne[164] because we think that it was he who originally suggested that she [Nancy] should work in the shop. That might forestall the C. pretending that she flew her in on her broomstick.

J.S.S.   9/11/73 (postcard)

Harold A. came to no. 10 for 45 mins. this morning, during 35 of which EHB was having his lunch. EF is always all over him for the first five mins., but I managed to talk to him downstairs without any upstairs suspicions being aroused. I simply warned him that [Mollie] was a Dangerous Woman, that she was in love with Nancy for some time and that her fully tabulated account will have a second side to it . . .

---

163. Harold Acton was preparing a book about Nancy Mitford, who had died in June. It was published in 1975.
164. James Lees-Milne (1908–97), diarist, one of the Hills' oldest friends.

H.H.   22/11/73

... about my Ritzy lunch, there is not really much to tell. I sat by the fountain at the appropriate time. A female figure in a brown top hat rose up, shouting my name. Nathalie Bevan.[165] She told me how she had been sitting there the day before when CMB came in, a large figure she said, who told her that she was all aflutter because she was helping HA with his book about Nancy. She was holding a sheaf of papers. (Oh Lord, what do they contain?) Nathalie took me over to Bobbie and they gave me a nice strong gin, which was a help. Harold soon arrived with his dancing step, admired the brown top hat and we were put at a tiny table by the entrance (he'd forgotten to book a table). He was extremely amiable and nice. Said hardly anything about CMB except some remark implying that he wasn't nuts about her ... I handed over my own sheaf, which was only a small red exercise book with a few funny bits from Nancy's letters. I didn't put in any of the violent postcards, which N. & M., at the height of their intimacy, used to send me, like "I hear that Mollie is leaving at the end of next week. In which case, so am I," though I confess to include one nasty thing (quoted from Nancy) "Evelyn says Handy has all the concealed malice of the natural underdog. Oh how I SCREAMED" ...

[Jacob Rothschild[166]] seemed to know quite a bit about the shop, that you are there and appreciated by the Bacons. Alarming in a way, isn't it, how the ripples of rumour come creeping out. ...

---

165. Mrs Nathalie Bevan, for many years Randolph Churchill's mistress. Her second husband was Robert (Bobby) Bevan, son of the Euston Road Group painter; he had run the advertising firm S. H. Benson.
166. Lord Rothschild (b. 1936), financier and patron.

J.S.S.   25/11/73

. . . a prize story, which comes from EHB, as told to Setitia. A porter in Barkston Gardens, who looks after one of the other blocks of flats (not 53), has taken it into his head to go at regular intervals to the pavement under Castle B. and shout "You're a bloody old bitch . . . everybody knows you're a bloody old bitch . . . I'm telling you you're a **BLOODY OLD BITCH.**" CMB cannot retaliate because she's afraid he'll go further. Handy has once gone out onto the balcony to face the abuse but has been prevented from shouting back for the same reason – he has merely peered dormouse-like at the pavement and tried to look like an extra fierce dormouse. Well, this is upsetting the Countess: "the Old Girl doesn't like it much, ha ha ha," and she has applied to Edward Dykes (their solicitor) for advice and legal aid. What can be done? Are you responsible for inspiring this noble, brave but fool-hardy character? If he's self-appointed, he deserves a platinum medal. But won't he be whisked away by an attack of magical appendicitis/heart-attack/stroke? . . .

. . . the new accounts girl disappeared to hospital for major treatment on her bunions and has been away, except for one day, since Nov. 1st. Mr Bacon has been doing some of her work, entering from the Day Book into ex-"my" ledgers, and has been learning a few home truths. Mark Wormald had major woman-trouble and after being jilted decided to go underground to have a break-down. He gave no notice and has not been heard of for a month. Liz is pointedly abdicating and simply suits herself about hours and work. She has had the grace not to antagonise more than her usual quota of customers because she's quite happy about the capability of Liz Archibald.[167] If she wasn't happy, it would be HELL. Liz

---

167. Elizabeth Archibald (b. 1951), a recent Cambridge graduate; later a distinguished medievalist and University don.

II is exceedingly competent, just what we need; I get on well with her and long may she stay. A new chap will be coming in January . . .

I rather forcibly told Derek Hill last week that I had considerable experience of two favourite murderer's weapons, the stiletto and the blunt instrument. Isn't he bound to describe Liz I as a blunt instrument to all his friends? . . .

Things are a bit gloomy because Laura's parents are in a very bad way and no one knows quite what's to be done[168] . . .

P.S. CMB to E.F. last Friday: "You *will* let me know if there's anything I can help with in the shop like delivering parcels or listing for Mr McMahon?" Are your withers wrung?

H.H.   3/12/73

The balcony scene from Handeo and Mollet is indeed a classic and I am infinitely grateful to you for writing it. Whatever can she have done to make the whole of Barkston rise against her, because certainly the porter must have been its mouthpiece? If only there was an EARLS COURT COURIER which could tell us the details.

We had lunch with Peggy Clutten one day last week, who, you will remember, was once CMB's headmistress. She told us how CMB was introduced to her by Betty Gwyer (now Mylius) and how she told her that she was Fröbel trained which made Peggy, to her lasting regret, book her as the maths mistress. The inevitable rows began and the resulting sparks even set fire to some of the parents who took their children away. When Peggy tried to sack her, she said if you do I will smash your furniture, ruin your school and tell all

---

168. Raymond Erith had just been admitted to the London Hospital for a lung operation from which he did not recover.

the parents that you are a HOMOsexual (her sorcery in those days must have been more crude). On another occasion she threatened to throw herself into the Thames (it was wartime and the school had been evacuated to near Henley). "What's more, you will have to jump in and save me" . . .

Rather to my dismay, I have come across a whole lot more letters from Nancy, which means I must be getting down to more homework for Harold . . .

1974

*Elizabeth Forbes left at Christmas 1973. With three-day
weeks and a series of strikes, the next few months were likely
to be a considerable challenge.*

H.H.   18/1/74

. . . I am sometimes asked by neighbours where they can
get some difficult book. When it's something like a Chinese
book on geo-physics, I usually, out of kindness, tell them to
go to John Sandoe (unless, of course, they are millionaires). I
stared at the shop window the other day when Anne and I
were in London for Antony [Gathorne-Hardy]'s *deuxième
noce* (a remarkable occurrence in Twickenham. Antony tot-
tered into the wrong flat, thinking that it was his bride's and
shouted at the astounded people "I am the groom." He imagined that they were his bride's relations). The shop looked
quite impenetrably dark – not that I thought of penetrating . . .

J.S.S.   27/1/74

. . . When you looked at no 10's window and saw how
much darkness reigned, you could have conceived the gloom
that these conditions have brought. We have electric light for
half days, morning one week and afternoon the next – , we're
allowed a full day's light on Saturday (ha! ha!) and all our
work, which never seems to stop, needs to be done, if possible, in half a day. In darkness we tend to put things off or put
things down – and yet be expected by customers to be our
normal happy selves – particularly when they ring up from
their fully-lit homes. Also with offices working only three
days, there's a greater than usual abundance of real nuts

around asking for daft books. Liz Archibald went down with pneumonia a week ago. Handy has taken his "long weekend" to coincide with her absence and Mr McMahon's been struck down with a cold. You can imagine what I feel like.

Handeo and Mollet was a tragedy, not a comedy. We had heard nothing more of the fate of the porter until Setitia asked Handy. "Oh" he said in his breeziest manner, "he was taken off to a bin. He'd made a lot of trouble all round, and the head porter and Mollie put their heads together and he was removed . . ."

When Mr McM., who lives alone, had not rung by 11 a.m. last Thursday, Handy said to Setitia: "I think the only thing will be for Mollie to go round to his rooms tomorrow morning and find out what's happened to him." To which Setitia said: "Handy, she *can't*, she's got nothing to do with the shop at all." Mr McMahon rang an hour later.

Setitia's going in mid-February and we've just found a nice girl to take her place. Nigel Palmer,[169] who started at the beginning of January, is 100% better than Mark ever was – he's been thrown into the deep end good and proper. He can have no conception of the change at HH since this time last year, and I won't tell him some of the harsher facts of the past for the time being. He has enjoyed his first three weeks, despite semi-darkness, and hasn't once had his head chopped off. Will he ever believe the truth about the Furies/Harpies? He asked Handy who you were during last week and this is what he was told:

"Well, you see I'm really Heywood Hill. I ran a bookshop in Curzon Street from 1930 onwards and, when someone else came along later in the 30s, we didn't think much of him, very little custom and absolutely no turnover. The shop was run by my wife and Nancy during the war, and then I came into it

---

169. Nigel Palmer (b. 1950), film lawyer since 1979.

immediately afterwards, etc. etc." This may sound incredible but HE ACTUALLY HAS COME TO BELIEVE IT HIMSELF.

He has offered, after his retirement, to stand in for me when I go on holiday. Mr Bacon and I have unanimously stalled.

In my next letter, of 17 February, I thanked Anne for sending a "riveting collection of papers". They referred to Mollie's earlier dismissals.[170] She felt she was indispensable and reckoned that, supported by Handy, she could outface her so-called boss. Anne also enclosed a hysterical letter [written in 1964] when Mollie was first told that Heywood was selling the shop to Henry Vyner. This included phrases like "you will know for the rest of your lives that you have ruined two lives".

Setitia had left the Friday before. Handy had shooed her into a waiting taxi at 4 p.m. when I was at Sotheby's, but she'd telephoned that evening to say that, although she would normally have been upset about leaving, the staff was not Heywood Hill as she had known it "for four and a half years", and "no tears were necessary".

That same day a lady customer aged around 50 had told Handy as she left, "I've talked now to all the people working in your shop. You're very lucky, they're all so charming. Are they all your family?"

Heywood had been choosing books for Mrs Mellon and, because he felt increasingly out of touch, hoped to have this burden removed – as long as I could take it on. He preferred to consult Mrs Mellon's London psychiatrist, Dr Carl Lambert, one of the most oblique people imaginable. The process inevitably became complicated . . .

---

170. Heywood had asked her to leave on five occasions, but she simply disregarded him; see page 34.

H.H. 16/4/74

It's extraordinary how nothing to do with the shop EVER seems to be straightforward. I don't imagine that it would be any help if Anne and I re-open accounts in the shop. Almost all we buy nowadays are a few odd paperbacks which would only be a nuisance. Then, on anything more expensive, there would be postage.[171]

J.S.S. 30/7/74

Might the dreaded Countess have seen you going into Harrods last Friday? This sounds like a question of Conse-quences, but your apparition made a considerable impact and I only hope you haven't started on some awful dreams. Handy had obviously been instructed to ask me what you now look like, which involved the vital question, when did you last see Heywood? So, with a month to succession-day, I risked all and said I'd seen you once or twice not so long ago – and as yet there have been no hideous results.

But can you imagine a Directors' Meeting tomorrow when Mr Bacon is expecting me to direct Handy into the rules and routines of future employment? "You will come in every Friday afternoon at precisely 2.30 p.m. and we do not expect you to have your hair cut during the two hours when you're meant to be working . . . You will CLEAR your desk within the next three weeks and leave it filth-less (what about Norman Hartnell's books about flagellation?[172]) for me to take it on for Sept. 1st. Et cetera.

Have I told you about the parties that are going to be given in Handy's honour? One by publishers' reps, at

---

171. They did re-open accounts and postage was never charged, in lieu of a "founder's discount".
172. Sir Norman Hartnell (1901–79), couturier. His copy of *Lure of the Rod* was in our packing room for twenty years, unread.

Bertorelli's in Sept. and the other during early October at William Collins's [office in St James's Place] by Messrs [Hamish] Hamilton, [Jock] Murray and [Sir William] Collins. Both had to be instigated and part-organised [by me] while H. was in the Dordogne, then presented to him as *faits accomplis*. He's allowed to ask exactly whom he likes of publishers and authors. "Of course my list reads like a roll-call from Who's Who, Lord and Lady Snow,[173] Lord and Lady Longford,[174] Lord and Lady Trevelyan,[175] Sir Harold Acton, etc." – what a fizzing chance to pay off old scores. The qualifications for an invitation, in case you are interested, are 1) Boots H. has licked; 2) Authors, *not* customers, who have burned incense at H.'s altar; 3) Anyone who doesn't know [the real] Mollie. Without any hope of success, I have suggested various people who ought to be there, e.g. Henry and Margaret Vyner, but they've been turned down out of hand: the Vs are "persona ingratissima" and it would be "wholly wrong that they should have lot or part in it".

H.H.   8/74 (undated)

Yes, Countess did see me going into Harrods on Thurs. (not Fri.) last week. I was going there to fill in time – before having lunch with Frances Partridge – by sitting among other elders in the lounge on the 4th floor. I wonder if she was in a bus or on foot. Just shows how thoroughly unsafe everything is. You really do deserve a medal for having confessed that you had seen me . . .

---

173. C. P. Snow (1905–80) and Pamela Hansford Johnson (1912–81), novelists.
174. Frank Pakenham, Lord Longford (1905–2001), and Elizabeth, née Harman (1906–2002), writers and parents of writers.
175. Lord Trevelyan (Humphrey) (1905–85) and his wife.

I long to hear how the directors' meeting of yesterday went off. Did Handy manage to do a bit of dodging? It reminded me of the meeting at Macfarlane's [his solicitors] with Handy, Henry and [Jeremy] Webster, when I was wound up, and told, obviously via the Countess – that I must on no account be allowed a key to the shop – and not conceivably be given a directorship.

I shall, of course, be gate-crashing the Who's Who party – dressed as a ghost.

H.H. 15/9/74
St Maxime, France, c/o Michael Behrens[176]

[Comments on Gerald Brenan's second volume of auto-biography, a proof of which I had sent for their holiday. Eddie Gathorne-Hardy had skimmed through it and said "he's conceited and a pathological liar, my dear," where Heywood thought that he "often got people wrong" and that it might "add fuel to the fire of the anti-Bloomsberries".]

. . . I do wonder how the Handy problem is for you. He must be so utterly lost without the shop and, what with the Witch of Barkston driving him out while she rides her Hoover, what refuge CAN there be – except the pub? . . .

J.S.S. 2/10/74

. . . At last a week's break and we're going to a Landmark Trust folly in Monmouthshire . . . By the time we come back, memories of the great Buchanan jamboree will have faded – probably because it wasn't extra-memorable. Handy was not drunk, Mollie didn't claw anyone's face and I didn't pass out with exhaustion – this was actually the most likely to happen because I caught some frightful bug last week and was feeling

---

176. Michael Behrens, banker and Harriet Hill's father-in-law.

exceptionally fragile. The cast included C. P. Snow, the Trevelyans, Sir P[hilip] Magnus,[177] Mrs Norman-Butler,[178] the Longfords, T. Driberg,[179] Margaret Lane,[180] Mrs Battiscombe,[181] the Powells;[182] golly, I can't think of any more. The Lees-Milnes didn't show up, and there were refusals from H. Acton, Joan Haslip, Lesley Blanch,[183] Cecil Woodham-Smith[184] and [Osbert] Lancaster. Publishers easily outweighed nob authors; average age about 64.

Mollie stood at the top of the stairs – leading to a very nice room in 14 St James's Place – , holding a couple of roses in her left hand and potentially ready to use the prickles. I just had time to mutter "Mollie" to Laura when we reached The Presence and she shook L.'s hand. No word about not having ever met before and, until we were about to leave, no further word to either of us. We weren't going to make any move towards her, but L. says that whenever she was within hearing distance, tangible rays of inquisitiveness came piercing through to her. Right at the end she sailed up to us – we'd had to wait to see the party breaking up – , and told me, cheerfully "I've just been talking for 20 minutes to someone I thought was George Weidenfeld and he turned out to be Max Reinhardt."[185] This did not lead to conversation.

W. Collins's speech had been *very* generous to the guest of honour: "I've known two great booksellers in my life, John

---

177. Sir Philip Magnus-Allcroft (1906–88), biographer.
178. Mrs Belinda Norman-Butler (b. 1908), W. M. Thackeray's great-granddaughter and a pillar of the English Speaking Union.
179. Lord Driberg (Tom) (1905–76), journalist.
180. Margaret Lane, Lady Huntingdon (1907–94), novelist and biographer.
181. Mrs Georgina Battiscombe (1904–2000), biographer.
182. Anthony Powell (1905–2005), novelist, and Lady Violet, née Pakenham (1912–2002), writer.
183. Lesley Blanch (b. 1905), writer, the only customer who started her letters "Darling Bookshop".
184. Cecil Woodham-Smith (1896–1977), historian.
185. Max Reinhardt (1905–2002), publisher.

Wilson of Bumpus, and H.B. It is cheering to know that H.'s shop will not be going the same way as Bumpus, but it obviously has a splendid future under etc etc. Handy is unique . . . He is not going to retire completely . . . Raise your glasses to Handy and Mollie."

Then Handy's reply: "No one who has known me in the shop would believe that in fact I am exceedingly shy. It is *very* kind of Billy (looking in the wrong direction), Jock and Jamie (looking in the wrong direction again) to have organised this party and of Billy to have made such a flattering speech. Of course a shop does not consist of one individual, nor could it ever do so. This is my chance to pay a proper tribute to my wife Mollie who did the shop's accounts for 30 years; to the indefatigable energy of Elizabeth Forbes, familiar to all visitors at no. 10 until Christmas last year; and of course, most important of all, to the flair and brilliance of my erstwhile partner, Heywood Hill." Loud cheers from all and DON'T YOU BELIEVE A WORD. He *actually* told them about two of his five-times-great-grandfathers being booksellers, both being Scots – a twinkling nudge to his three hosts – , and the Excitement of having been a Bookseller all his life. I could give you the exact words but you will have heard that record often before.

The next morning he definitely reckoned it had been a Success and I think most of the guests would have agreed. Tom Driberg was amazed at how coherent he had been, and at such a late hour of night. Further reactions will doubtless be heard in the next few days.

H.H.   18/10/74

[Thank you for] your riveting account of THE LAST JAMBOREE. I can't get over the thought of those two roses and am certain I shall dream about them. Thank heavens that

Laura managed to avoid being pricked by the thorns. I feel that she was in GREAT danger. She'd have needed a very professional fairy Godmother to undo the spell. Even I have not found one yet.

In my next letter, dated 1 November, I admitted to a dearth of "horror stories; not a squeak from Mollie, not a shadow of the grand Lady of the Opera, but far too much of Handy". His half-day every week was an indulgence for him, and a crashing bore for the rest of us. During my holiday he had charged "expenses" for his journey to and from Earls Court, a principle which I told him was "disgraceful". This was at first denied and he then reverted to "aggressive dodging": "I've talked it over with the owner and it won't happen again."

The recession was obviously biting but we were very busy and "it does make a difference when everyone in the shop is HAPPY".

Heywood's final letter of the year was dated 27 November. "I did laugh about you calling Handy a disgrace. I can still hear that noise of his shovelling handfuls of 'expenses' out of the till and remember how it used to make me boil (though I was too deplorably meek to boil over). I ought to have done a bit more shovelling myself but Anne and I, when we began, had so disciplined ourselves to shoe strings (the shop would never have survived if we had not) that I could not do it."

EPILOGUE

Heywood and I continued to correspond until his death. Once Handy Buchanan had completed his period of semi-retirement when he appeared in the shop for half a day a week, the horror stories lost their savour. I asked him in 1975 if he'd like to compile a stock catalogue. He insisted that I should choose the books, and that he should be paid by the hour. For several weeks, when I'd locked up at Saturday lunchtime, I left him books on a desk downstairs. I imagined that he would work on them for an hour or more, checking details from our considerable library of bibliography. During one such afternoon, I rang him when I got home because I thought I might not have put the till in the safe; only half an hour had passed since I'd left, but he'd already left for the pub. The cataloguing was paid for but his efforts never reached printed form.

Handy was commissioned by Weidenfeld and Nicolson to write an illustrated book on natural history books. It was published in 1979 under the title *Nature Into Art*. His personal books were sold through auction rooms: his presentation copies at Sotheby's during the 1980s, the rest at Bloomsbury Book Auctions in 2002. I described the latter for Susan Hill's last issue of Books and Company: seeing them grouped together on an auctioneer's shelves had provoked many early memories, not least of his Last Jamboree. For this occasion he had been given a special copy of Kenneth Clark's *Moments of Vision* which had been signed by the guests and inscribed "To Handasyde, a token of affection, gratitude and good wishes." At the auction we failed to buy it.

After Handy's death in 1984, Mollie moved from Bark-ston Gardens to a smaller flat in Onslow Gardens sw7, where she lived until she went to a retirement home in Roehampton. She died, aged 96, in 2005.

Heywood lived in Snape Priory until he died, in 1986. Anne continues to live there, with her daughter Harriet and her son-in-law Simon Frazer.

ACKNOWLEDGEMENTS

This book was typed from my longhand by Kirsty Anderson; I owe her a great debt of gratitude. I owe a similar debt to my enthusiastic publisher, John Nicoll, and my supportive editor, Jane Havell. Footnotes and family trees could not have been completed without the help of James Fergusson and Harriet Frazer; I am also grateful to Harriet and her mother Lady Anne Hill for allowing me to use my letters which they have kept safe for more than thirty years.

For my wife Laura, who vividly remembers many of the events described, I reserve my warmest and most affectionate thanks.

BIOGRAPHICAL INDEX

HANDASYDE BUCHANAN (1907–84) Educated at Rugby and University College, Oxford. Worked for Michael Williams at 3 Curzon Street from 1930 to 1940. In Press Censorship until 1945 when he was invited to join Heywood Hill. Managed the shop from 1965 to his retirement in 1974.

MOLLIE BUCHANAN (1909–2005), née Catleugh, then Friese-Green. Started at Heywood Hill in 1943, running the accounts, and helped Nancy Mitford to keep it going until 1945. Married Handy in 1949; worked for the shop until 1973.

ELIZABETH FORBES (b. 1924) Bookseller and music columnist. Worked for Heywood Hill between 1946 and 1973 when she left to become an opera critic.

LADY ANNE HILL (b. 1911) The younger sister of four Gathorne-Hardy brothers, she married Heywood Hill in 1938. Mother of Harriet and Lucy.

HARRIET HILL (b. 1943) Heywood and Anne's older daughter. Married Tim Behrens, artist, in 1963 and had three children; then Simon Frazer. After the death of her step-daughter Sophie in 1985, she founded Memorials by Artists.

HEYWOOD HILL (1906–86) Educated at Eton and (briefly) Cambridge. Apprenticed to Charles Sawyer 1930–36; founded bookshop in September 1936; called up in December 1942; retired full-time in 1965.

LUCY HILL (b. 1946) Younger daughter of Heywood and Anne. Married Geordie Redpath in 1970; five children.

JOHN SAUMAREZ SMITH (b. 1943) Eldest of four children of Bill and Betty Saumarez Smith. Educated at Winchester and Trinity College, Cambridge; joined Heywood Hill in 1965.

LAURA SAUMAREZ SMITH (b. 1945) The youngest of four daughters of Raymond and Pamela Erith. Brought up in Dedham; married John in 1969; had two sons, Joseph and George; now grandmother of three.

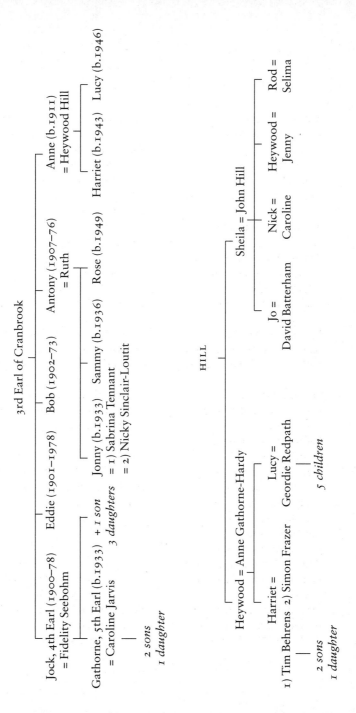

GATHORNE-HARDY

3rd Earl of Cranbrook

Jock, 4th Earl (1900–78)
= Fidelity Seebohm

Eddie (1901–1978)

Bob (1902–73)

Antony (1907–76)
= Ruth

Anne (b.1911)
= Heywood Hill

Gathorne, 5th Earl (b.1933) + 1 son
= Caroline Jarvis   3 daughters

Jonny (b.1933)   Sammy (b.1936)
= 1) Sabrina Tennant
= 2) Nicky Sinclair-Loutit

Rose (b.1949)

Harriet (b.1943)   Lucy (b.1946)

2 sons
1 daughter

HILL

Sheila = John Hill

Heywood = Anne Gathorne-Hardy

Jo =
David Batterham

Nick =
Caroline

Heywood =
Jenny

Rod =
Selima

Harriet =
1) Tim Behrens 2) Simon Frazer

Lucy =
Geordie Redpath

2 sons
1 daughter

5 children

INDEX